EARLY CHILDHOOD EDUCATION SERIES
Leslie R. Williams, Editor

ADVISORY BOARD: Barbara T. Bowman, Harriet K. Cuffaro, Stephanie Feeney,
Doris Pronin Fromberg, Celia Genishi, Stacie G. Goffin, Dominic F. Gullo,
Alice Sterling Honig, Elizabeth Jones, Gwen Morgan

(continued)

Enthusiastic and Engaged Learners

Approaches to Learning in the Early Childhood Classroom

MARILOU HYSON

Foreword by Sue Bredekamp

Teachers College
Columbia University
New York and London

National Association
for the Education of
Young Children

Credits, chapter opening photos: pages 1, 9, 30, © Karen Phillips; pages 20, 122, © Shari Schmidt; page 44, Marilyn Nolt, noltphotos@mail.com; page 57, William Geiger/© NAEYC; page 69, Barbara Bent/© NAEYC; page 84, photo by Penny Farster-Narlesky; page 96, © Elisabeth Nichols; page 111, © Ellen B. Senisi.

Published simultaneously by Teachers College Press, 1234 Amsterdam Avenue, New York, NY 10027 and the National Association for the Education of Young Children, 1313 L Street NW, Suite 500, Washington, DC 20005

Library of Congress Cataloging-in-Publication Data

Hyson, Marilou.
    Enthusiastic and engaged learners : approaches to learning in the early childhood classroom / Marilou Hyson.
        p.   cm. — (Early childhood education series)
Includes bibliographical references and index.
ISBN 978-0-8077-4880-0 (pbk. : alk. paper)
    1. Early childhood education—United States.   2. Learning strategies—United States.   3. Motivation in education—United States.   I. Title.

    LB1139.25.H965   2008
    372.21—dc22   2008011040

ISBN 978-0-8077-4880-0 (paper)

NAEYC item 733

Printed on acid-free paper
Manufactured in the United States of America

15   14   13   12   11   10   09   08   8   7   6   5   4   3   2   1

Contents

Foreword

N WRITING A FOREWORD, it is often useful to begin by looking backward. Almost two decades ago, the President and the nation's governors established a set of National Education Goals, the first of which was, "By the year 2000, all children will start school ready to learn." I served as a member of the Goal 1 Technical Planning Group, whose charge was to define the broad term "school readiness." With the clarity of hindsight, I now think that the group was brilliant in including *approaches to learning* in their multidimensional definition (Kagan, Moore, & Bredekamp, 1995).

Admittedly, we weren't exactly certain what this dimension included, and little research existed to justify its importance. Nevertheless, knowledgeable early childhood professionals valued positive approaches to learning. And like other aspects of "quality," we knew it when we saw it, so to speak. In the intervening years, however, children's approaches to learning continued to receive less attention than they deserved.

Recently, however, teachers and parents have become quite concerned that an overemphasis on standardized test scores in reading and mathematics is damaging children's motivation and interest in education. In light of the current context and our expanding knowledge base, Marilou Hyson's excellent book could not come at a more opportune moment in the history of early childhood education.

This book fills a void that has existed in the field for some time. As someone who has grappled with the thorny challenge of definition, I find enormous value in the conceptual organization and definitional clarity that Hyson lends to the heretofore loosely conceived construct approaches to learning. She points out the many different terms that have been used for the various concepts and helps the reader understand how they are synonymous or distinct.

In addition, by compiling the relevant research across these dimensions, Hyson documents evidence-based practices for promoting positive approaches to learning in all children, as well as intervening with disengaged or uninterested children. At the same time, she articulates the gaps in the knowledge base, thus setting forth a research agenda for the future.

In dispelling some of the myths related to the role of heredity, this book will help teachers better understand the origins of various approaches to learning. Hyson describes how children have inborn tendencies that influence their temperaments and self-regulation capacities. But she also clearly explains how these approaches to learning are amenable to intervention and intentional teaching.

Hyson has truly given early childhood educators a great gift. We will now have *Enthusiastic and Engaged Learners* as a framework to guide our understanding and communication about approaches to learning. In those two words, *enthusiastic* and *engaged*, Hyson captures not only the complexity of children's approaches to learning but also the essence of their interconnectedness. Her message is clear: Effective learning requires activation of *both* positive emotions and motivation *and* engaged actions and behaviors, including attention, persistence, flexibility, and self-regulation. *Enthusiastic* and *engaged* are not the primary learning goals, but instead they are a means to an end—enhanced achievement across all areas of the curriculum and a disposition toward life-long learning. In short, fun for fun's sake is inadequate, as is the assumption that learning can result without attention to pleasure and interest.

The practical tools and specific recommendations are what make this book so useful. These *nuts and bolts* suggestions include ways to

1. build supportive relationships with individual children necessary for understanding their various approaches to learning;
2. adapt curriculum to enhance motivation and engagement;
3. implement specific teaching strategies that build motivation and enthusiasm, as well as engagement in learning tasks;
4. assess children's approaches to learning accurately;
5. work with families to better understand children, their cultural backgrounds, and their individual needs, and to promote positive approaches to learning through partnerships; and
6. advocate for inclusion of positive approaches to learning in all relevant educational policies.

Throughout this book, the author appropriately qualifies many conclusions in light of the realities of cultural and linguistic differences. In addition, she fully includes attention to children with disabilities and special needs.

Lively and enchanting vignettes of children, teachers, and classrooms abound in this book, thus bringing to life the theoretical constructs explored. In addition, the author's clear, concrete, and well-organized writing style keeps the reader enthusiastic and engaged throughout.

Marilou Hyson is one of the most enthusiastic and engaged learners I've ever encountered in the early childhood profession. By that I mean that she continually embraces new knowledge and is willing to learn and change her perspectives. She also has an exceptional ability to produce new knowledge as well as communicate and disseminate it widely to diverse audiences. At the same time, she never loses her own enthusiasm for the unbridled, unique joy that only young children can bring to our lives. I am truly glad and grateful that she has expanded and deepened the work begun so long ago by the Goal 1 group. By comprehending the critical role of children's positive approaches to learning, early childhood professionals' own enthusiasm and engagement in their work can only be enhanced.

—Sue Bredekamp

Acknowledgments

ALTHOUGH MINE IS THE ONLY NAME on the cover, *Enthusiastic and Engaged Learners* was not a solo effort. I thank Teachers College Press, especially Marie Ellen Larcada, for encouraging me to pursue this idea, as well as the many friends and colleagues who said, "*Yes*, we really need a book like this, and I'm so glad I don't have to write it!"

All of us in the early childhood field are indebted to the National Education Goals Panel's Goal 1 Technical Planning Group, notably the conceptual leadership of Sue Bredekamp, Lilian Katz, Evelyn Moore, and Sharon Lynn Kagan, who in the 1990s identified and wrote about approaches to learning as a key dimension of school readiness. I have also admired and drawn upon work by scholars too numerous to mention. Some of those whose research has strongly influenced my thinking are Clancy Blair, Elena Bodrova and Debbie Leong, Carol Dweck, John Fantuzzo, Adele Gottfried, John Guthrie, Carroll Izard, Megan McClelland, Robin McWilliam, Fred Morrison, Bob Pianta, Cybele Raver, Ann Renninger, Catherine Scott-Little, Deborah Stipek, and Alan Wigfield. With their research collaborators, they continue to provide new insights into the development of, and influences on, various components of children's enthusiasm for and engagement in learning.

Yet this scholarship would lack relevance without a solid grounding in the world of early childhood practice. In this book I provide many vignettes and brief examples from early childhood programs. Some of these examples draw on my observations in different programs over the years as a teacher, researcher, teacher educator, and professional development specialist. Other examples have been based on visits to early childhood programs that generously invited me to do observations specifically for this book. For this opportunity, and for the inspiration that their teachers, administrators, and children embody, I sincerely thank CentroNia DC Bilingual Public Charter School in Washington, DC; Charlestown Play House in Phoenixville, PA; the School for Friends in Washington, DC; and Summerfield School, Neptune Township, NJ. When using material from these observations, I have changed details to ensure privacy for programs, teachers, and children; to illustrate specific points more clearly, I have sometimes altered details or combined elements from different observations.

Also richly deserving of thanks are my professional colleagues, including treasured friends at the National Association for the Education of Young Children (NAEYC), as well as those at the National Association of Early Childhood

Specialists in State Departments of Education, at the Society for Research in Child Development, and at the Division for Early Childhood of the Council for Exceptional Children. Their insights into practice and policy issues have helped me to better understand the complicated "circles of influence" on children's approaches to learning. Additionally, I value the interactions I have had with my co-presenters at the NAEYC Professional Development Institute, June 2007: Margaret Annunziata, Dina Clark, Elisa Huss-Hage, and Julie Ray. Their thoughts about how enthusiasm and engagement can be both supported and undermined moved the conference participants and gave me much to think about. I also want to make special mention of Janis Keyser's writing on family-centered early childhood education, which greatly influenced Chapter 9, and Adele Robinson's work on policy advocacy, which informed major sections of Chapter 10. The influence of the late Leslie Williams, Editor of Teachers College Press's Early Childhood Education Series, is reflected in this book and in the many publications developed under her leadership. She is greatly missed.

Even with all this help, bridging the gap between a draft manuscript and a finished book would have been impossible without Susan Liddicoat's skilled and tactful editing; Patrick Cavanagh's transformation of my kindergarten-looking diagrams into professional illustrations; Lisa Cook's eagle-eyed reference checks and formatting assistance; and Sam Hyson's ability to read my tiny handwriting and "Accept All Changes" in a document.

Finally, of course, I gratefully acknowledge my family—John, Dan, Jess, Jeff, Juliette, Sam, and Ellie—for their enthusiasm, engagement, and patience with this book, even during periods of my excessive immersion; and for the way that all of them embody enthusiasm and engagement in their own lives and work.

Introduction

It is the first week of kindergarten, and Leon and Joe are at the puzzle table. Leon has chosen an especially difficult animal puzzle, and his brow wrinkles in concentration as he looks first at the picture on the puzzle box and then at the pieces on the table, paying little attention to the chatter of other children as they arrive. He lines up the pieces, choosing one and carefully moving it into what he thinks is the right position. When it doesn't fit after several tries, Leon puts it aside and tries another piece that looks similar but is slightly different in shape. Leaning forward expectantly, he turns the piece one way and then another, finally finding the right placement. "It fits!" he calls to his teacher, and with a broad smile he reaches for the next piece. Persisting until he finishes the puzzle, he picks up one of the pieces—an elephant—and "dances" it across the table toward his friend Joe.

Next to Leon, Joe sits slumped in his chair. He came to the table only after protesting to the teacher, "But I don't know how to do these puzzles." Once seated, Joe selects a puzzle, begins to work on it, but then gives up quickly when he can't figure out where one of the pieces should go. Now he waits passively for someone to tell him what else he can do in the classroom.

LEON AND JOE already show very different *approaches to learning*—the motivations, attitudes, and behaviors that children display when participating in educational activities. In contrast to Joe's manner, Leon appears confident, curious, persistent, and eager to take on new learning challenges. Increasingly, researchers are finding that these kinds of attitudes and learning behaviors underlie children's ability to learn and succeed in school.

The term "approaches to learning" first emerged from the work of the National Education Goals Panel, established in 1990 to assess and report on progress toward six goals, the first of which was that all children should start school ready to learn. In one of the reports from the Goal 1 Technical Planning Group, Kagan, Moore, and Bredekamp (1995) described approaches to learning as one of the key dimensions of school readiness. In fact, the authors stated that "of all the school readiness domains, Approaches to Learning is the least understood, the least researched, and perhaps the most important dimension" (p. 22). These attitudes, dispositions, or learning behaviors are now regarded as critical underpinnings for school success.

WHAT WE KNOW ABOUT APPROACHES TO LEARNING

Kagan et al. (1995), the National Education Goals Panel (1997), the National Center for Education Statistics (2002), and others have described approaches to learning in terms of multiple components. Many of these are evident in Leon's behavior.

- *Intrinsic motivation to learn.* Faced with a number of choices during this part of the morning schedule, Leon selected a difficult puzzle—not because he had to, but because of his desire to master the challenge.
- *Interest and joy in learning.* Leon's face, voice, body language, and the choices he makes show that he already has a curious, eager attitude toward learning. He is always wondering *how* and *why* and is often the first to volunteer for a new experience.
- *Engagement.* Leon becomes deeply involved in his work with the puzzle.
- *Persistence.* Leon sticks with the puzzle for a long period of time.
- *Planning.* Leon's strategies for solving the puzzle show that he plans ahead, pondering how to go about working on the puzzle before jumping in.
- *Ability to focus and control attention.* The room is noisy as children continue to come in and begin the morning's work, but Leon is able to attend to the task he has chosen, looking up at his friends but continuing to focus on finishing the puzzle.
- *Flexible problem-solving.* Leon tries some new approaches after he is unable to make one piece fit as he had thought it would.

◆ *Inventiveness.* Even when doing something like a puzzle, which has one correct solution, Leon shows his creative streak, playfully making a puzzle piece do a dance on the table.

◆ *Tolerance for frustration.* When Leon can't make the pieces fit, he does not collapse into avoidance, anger, or apathy. He may not be happy about his inability to solve the puzzle, but he regulates his emotional state and behavior, getting through the difficulty and ultimately experiencing success.

Going beyond the components of approaches to learning, research is clear on at least five points:

1. Children begin to develop these characteristics and behaviors at an early age.
2. Even in the early years, children differ in their approaches to learning.
3. These differences influence children's school readiness and school success.
4. Children's experiences at home and in early childhood programs can strengthen or undermine their positive approaches to learning.
5. Early childhood programs can implement specific strategies that will promote positive approaches to learning in areas such as strengthening relationships with children, working together with families, designing supportive classroom environments, and selecting effective curriculum and teaching methods.

WHY A BOOK ON APPROACHES TO LEARNING? WHY NOW?

Despite the research on many of the specific components of approaches to learning, and despite the critical significance of these dimensions of early development and learning, we are just beginning to put together the key findings and their implications for practice and for educational policies.

Growing Interest in Approaches to Learning . . .

Early childhood professionals know that children's approaches to learning are important. Teachers, teacher educators, and others are looking for specific evidence to support their commitment to developing positive approaches to learning. They are also looking for research-based strategies to use in their classrooms, to recommend in their teacher preparation programs, or to use in policy advocacy. A number of states have intentionally included the domain of approaches to learning in their early learning standards; Head Start, too, has incorporated this aspect of school readiness into its child outcomes framework. Researchers have begun to make progress not only in expanding understanding of approaches to learning but also in developing assessments and classroom-based interventions.

Additionally, NAEYC's new standards and accreditation criteria for early childhood programs explicitly name approaches to learning as an area of emphasis in high-quality programs.

. . . But Multiple Risks for Children

Despite these promising trends, today young children's interest, engagement, persistence, and motivation are being placed at risk—which, in turn, places at risk children's future success and satisfaction with learning. Some of these risks come from the challenges of poverty, violence, and instability within families and communities. Other risks are related to trends in early childhood curriculum, teaching, and assessment practices that together may undermine rather than strengthen positive approaches to learning. Frequently discussed is the impact of high-stakes testing, with a resulting emphasis on a narrow range of academic goals and a heightened emphasis on extrinsic rewards and sanctions for performance. Risks also arise from the inadequate supply of evidence-based early childhood professional development, limiting teachers' ability to create the high-quality programs that will support children's positive approaches to learning. The risks are many, but so are the remedies. Action is needed to remove barriers and to direct greater attention to approaches to learning.

USING THIS BOOK

In this book, which is organized into two parts, I aim to help current and future early childhood educators and education decision makers implement strategies to support positive approaches to learning for all children. Here the greatest emphasis is on children ages 3–6. However, the foundations of positive approaches to learning are established earlier, and their effects continue into and beyond the early grades of school. Following this Introduction, the chapters in Part I describe a conceptual framework and evidence base for the meaning, importance, and major influences on young children's approaches to learning. In Part II, the chapters present specific tools that early childhood educators can use to ensure effective attention to this domain of development and learning. I hope that the book's content, organization, and resources will help you become better able to

- Define and describe young children's approaches to learning
- Know what research says about why approaches to learning are so important
- Understand how children acquire positive approaches to learning, and what may undermine these important aspects of school readiness
- Consider cultural and individual issues when assessing and promoting positive children's approaches to learning and when working with families

- Identify and plan specific strategies to increase positive approaches to learning
- Select and use assessments of children's approaches to learning to plan interventions
- Learn how to modify curriculum and teaching practices to create expanded opportunities to promote positive approaches to learning
- Become familiar with resources to help every child enter school with positive approaches to learning
- Advocate for more attention to children's approaches to learning in educational policies and decision-making

Enthusiastic and Engaged Learners has a number of features intended to support readers' own engagement in, and application of, the ideas presented. Throughout the book I offer numerous vignettes from early childhood programs. These are not intended to serve as perfect examples but rather to illustrate the realities and challenges of strengthening young children's approaches to learning. Also woven throughout the book are practical resources to help readers reflect on and apply their emerging knowledge about approaches to learning. Appendices include a developmental continuum for approaches to learning and an Action Planning Form to help readers put the book's ideas into practice. In addition, I begin each chapter with a set of goals, and I end each chapter with a list of activities to promote reflection, discussion, and action. Faculty or those doing community training may wish to use these to catalyze group interactions or as a basis for course assignments.

GETTING STARTED

As a reader, you will get more out of this book if you begin with an attitude of enthusiasm and engagement. I invite you to preview the chapters and see what captures your interest most strongly or what is most meaningful to you, reflecting on why that may be so. If possible, do this with fellow students or colleagues. As you get started, you might consider these questions:

- What, in your own life, have been the experiences that sparked your interest?
- When did you learn best—with the greatest engagement and depth?
- What helps you be a motivated and committed learner?
- What is your own style of learning, and how can you tap into that to further your own professional growth?

As you begin learning more about young children's approaches to learning, you will undoubtedly learn more about yourself. Best wishes as you begin this journey!

PART I

Setting the Stage for Action
Four Questions to Consider

To be prepared to take effective action that will support children's positive approaches to learning, early childhood educators should begin by considering answers to the four key questions posed by the titles of the chapters in Part I.

- First we need clear, consistent descriptions of children's positive approaches to learning. In Chapter 1 I review the history of the concept and the many ways in which approaches to learning have been defined and categorized.
- Then we need to be able to describe why these positive approaches to learning are so important to children's development. Chapter 2 provides persuasive evidence of these contributions.
- Next we need to appreciate the range of influences on these approaches to learning—extending from children's individual characteristics to the cultural, social, and political contexts in which they live. In Chapter 3 I summarize research on some of these influences.
- Finally, effective action depends on a realistic understanding of the factors that are currently putting children's enthusiasm and engagement at serious risk. Chapter 4 analyzes these factors.

By addressing these questions, the four chapters in Part I set the stage for Part II, where I suggest specific tools and action steps to use within and beyond early childhood education programs.

1 What Are Positive Approaches to Learning?

- *Monica has been sitting alone at one of the art tables for at least 15 minutes. The 4-year-old has been working steadily, experimenting with dripping different colors onto circles of coffee filter paper. As she works, her facial expressions gradually shift from serious concentration to puzzled frowns to little smiles of satisfaction to surprise when her dripping technique produces an unexpected effect.*
- *Charles and Joshua, who are almost 3, sit side by side on bouncing horses in a corner of the room. Both are bouncing rhythmically; as they bounce, they look at each other and smile occasionally. Every once in a while, one of the children varies the riding technique—bouncing slower or faster, or standing up a bit in the saddle. Then the other child looks over, pauses, and imitates the variation. The turn-taking and imitation continue for a long time.*
- *In a family child care home, four children ranging from 18 months to 5 years are outdoors in the sandbox. Together they are digging a large hole, using their hands and small shovels. Judging by the size of the hole, they have been at it for quite a while. Emma, the family child care provider, comes over to tell the children that it is time to come in and get ready for lunch. "But we're working," the oldest child protests.*

◆ *During the morning in a prekindergarten group, the teachers have set up several tables with open-ended art activities. Gus takes paper and crayons and starts to draw a person, making a round head and round body. He sits, pauses and ponders, and then snaps his fingers as if he has just thought of something. He slowly adds two arms and hands to the picture, and then sits again looking at what he has done. A visiting parent asks, "Are you tired today, Gus?" "No," he answers. "I'm just thinking."*

◆ *A class of kindergartners is playing a game. Two at a time, children work together to keep a large ball in place between their foreheads as they walk together to the other end of the rug without touching the ball. Everyone's focus is on the children as they try to succeed at this challenging task.*

EACH OF THESE EXAMPLES shows children using positive approaches to learning. But what exactly do we mean by "approaches to learning"? What specific feelings, behaviors, and tendencies are part of this essential aspect of early childhood development?

This chapter begins by introducing readers to the concept of approaches to learning. I will discuss the origins of the term, situating it within the larger context of school readiness and the work of the National Education Goals Panel (NEGP). Next I will explore the ways that approaches to learning and related terms have been defined. Then I will focus on the many feelings, motivations, attitudes, and behaviors that could be considered part of approaches to learning. To organize these components in a meaningful way, I propose an approaches-to-learning framework that will be used throughout the book.

 Goals of This Chapter

After reading this chapter, you will be better able to

1. Explain to others where the idea of approaches to learning came from, what the term means, and how it connects to other, similar terms.

2. Understand the various components of children's approaches to learning.

3. Critically analyze the suggested approaches-to-learning framework.

THE CONCEPT OF APPROACHES TO LEARNING— SOME HISTORICAL BACKGROUND

As suggested in the Introduction, "approaches to learning" has come to be used as a kind of shorthand phrase to describe behaviors, tendencies, or typical patterns that children use in learning situations—such as curiosity, persistence, and flexibility in solving problems. By looking briefly at some recent history, we can understand the reasons behind the use of this concept in early childhood education.

The Context of School Readiness and the National Education Goals

Although "school readiness" was much discussed during the 1950s and 1960s (Meisels, 1999; Vinovskis, 1995), the most recent version of the U.S. focus on school readiness began in the 1980s, following release of the report *A Nation at Risk* (U.S. Department of Education, 1983). That report described a "rising tide of mediocrity" in the nation's schools and warned that this would put the United States at a competitive disadvantage in comparison with other countries. Motivated by that warning, in 1989 President G. H. W. Bush and the state governors convened an education summit. The summit resulted in six broad national education goals, later expanded to eight, and challenged the nation to achieve these goals by the year 2000. At the same time, the NEGP was formed to assess and monitor progress toward the goals. The goals and their rationale were published under the title *The National Education Goals Report: Building a Nation of Learners, 1991* (National Education Goals Panel, 1991). In 1994 Congress enacted the *Goals 2000: Educate America Act*. Although the year 2000 passed without successful accomplishment of the goals, and although the NEGP's work terminated in 2002, the goals have continued to influence many federal and state discussions about the future of American education.

As defined by the governors and administration, and approved by Congress, the first National Education Goal was "School Readiness." Specifically, Goal 1 stated that "By the year 2000, all children in America will start school ready to learn." Many experts in early childhood development and education applauded the emphasis on the early years but disagreed with the implication that learning does not begin until children start school. A Goal 1 Technical Planning Group on Readiness for School was appointed, with members including national leaders in early childhood research, policy, and practice. Their task was to further flesh out the concepts of "ready to learn" and "school readiness." Deliberately, this group chose not to use the term "readiness" and instead defined five dimensions of "early development and learning" that "contribute significantly to children's success in formal school" (NEGP, 1997, p. 3).

The NEGP's "Approaches Toward Learning" as an Essential Dimension of Early Development and Learning

The NEGP's Goal 1 Technical Planning Group defined the dimensions of early development and learning (what many referred to as school readiness) as follows: (1) Physical Well-Being and Motor Development; (2) Social and Emotional Development; (3) Approaches Toward Learning; (4) Language Development; and (5) Cognition and General Knowledge (Kagan et al., 1995).

Although the other dimensions had been commonly included in previous descriptions of school readiness and early learning, the Goal 1 Technical Planning Group appears to have coined a new phrase for the early childhood field when it added "Approaches Toward Learning" as the third of its five dimensions. The reason for this addition was that the Technical Planning Group strongly believed that the "mere acquisition of knowledge, skills, and capacities is an insufficient criterion of developmental success. . . . Children must be *inclined* to marshal such skills and capacities" (Kagan et al., 1995, p. 23). It was this "inclination" that the Goal 1 Technical Planning Group intended to capture in the phrase Approaches Toward Learning (which I will call "approaches *to* learning," following the more frequent subsequent usage). Influenced by children's early and sometimes inborn predispositions, approaches to learning refers to "how children approach learning situations—their *learning styles* . . . aggregated variables that characterize ways of responding across situations" (Kagan et al., p. 23). In other words, approaches to learning describes not the *what* but the *how* of learning. In the examples at the beginning of the chapter, the main point is not Gus's drawing ability, but *how* Gus stops and thinks as he plans to draw his person; it is not whether the kindergartners can successfully walk across the room holding the ball between their foreheads, but *how* the pairs of children eagerly and planfully rise to this new challenge together.

COMPARING APPROACHES TO LEARNING WITH OTHER UMBRELLA TERMS

The Goal 1 Technical Planning Group considered their phrase Approaches Toward Learning "an umbrella term covering a range of attitudes, habits, and learning styles" (Kagan et al., 1995, p. 23). Yet other umbrella terms or broad designations could also be used to describe these kinds of qualities. Here I will briefly define three of these: "dispositions," "learning behaviors," and "learning-related skills."

Dispositions

In several publications, Lilian Katz (1991, 1995) has used the term "dispositions" in ways that are similar to the ideas behind the term "approaches to learning." She has emphasized that—along with knowledge, skills, and feelings—"dispositions" should be included among the important goals of any curriculum, of education in general, and of early childhood education in particular.

Learning Behaviors

The phrase "learning behaviors" is another example of an umbrella term for this aspect of children's development and learning. Fantuzzo and colleagues define approaches to learning in terms of "distinct sets of behaviors that indicate ways that children become engaged in classroom learning activities" (Fantuzzo, Perry, & McDermott, 2004, p. 213). In their work, they often call these "learning behaviors" rather than "approaches to learning," thereby emphasizing observable, measurable behaviors. The research group emphasizes that these learning behaviors are not only important for academic success but are also able to be strengthened through well-planned curriculum and teaching strategies (Rouse & Fantuzzo, 2008).

Learning-Related Skills

Another group of researchers (McClelland, Acock, & Morrison, 2006) has used still another umbrella term: "Learning-Related Skills," which they called "Learning-Related Social Skills" in their earlier publications (e.g., McClelland & Morrison, 2003). In their work, the phrase covers a number of characteristics such as self-control, cooperation, assertion, planning, and self-regulation skills.

Selecting the Umbrella Term for This Book

Although these and other umbrella terms are reasonable alternatives, I will use the term "approaches to learning" as the primary way of referring to this domain of early development and learning. The term has several advantages. First, it emerged from, and continues to be closely connected with, discussions of early childhood development and school readiness (e.g., Chen & McNamee, 2007; Fantuzzo et al., 2004). Second, it has been used by a number of states as a key dimension of their early learning standards and school readiness initiatives, and in a major analysis of the content of state early learning standards (Scott-Little, Kagan, & Frelow, 2005). Finally, in developing its Child Outcomes Framework, the Head Start Bureau (2001) has used the term approaches to learning to describe one of the framework's eight domains or categories.

But if we are going to pick up the approaches-to-learning umbrella, we will have to heed a few cautions. There is no single, universal definition of approaches to learning. For example, some people seem to use the term approaches to learning as a way of emphasizing children's inborn differences in temperament or learning styles; in contrast, others seem to stress that children's approaches to learning are behaviors that can be taught and changed over time. And sometimes the phrase has been used so broadly as to be meaningless.

Keeping these cautions in mind, I will use approaches to learning as this book's umbrella term while drawing upon valuable related concepts and terminology.

STEPS TOWARD A CONCEPT OF YOUNG CHILDREN'S APPROACHES TO LEARNING

Satisfactory as the term approaches to learning may be for general purposes, the umbrella is not enough. Without a clear description of the components of approaches to learning, the term does not give early childhood educators enough precise content.

Creating Lists of Components

The NEGP's Goal 1 Technical Planning Group specified five components or aspects of approaches to learning: "openness to and curiosity about new tasks and challenges; initiative, task persistence, and attentiveness; approach to reflection and interpretation; capacity for invention and imagination; and cognitive approaches to tasks." Together, these were referred to as "variables that affect how children approach learning situations" (Kagan et al., 1995, p. 23). Their report briefly describes each of these "learning styles." Looking back at the vignettes at the beginning of this chapter, it is easy to find examples of each.

Although the NEGP list continues to be deservedly influential and widely used, over the years many groups and individuals have expanded, reworded, and reframed this list. Additionally, developmental and educational researchers have investigated many other constructs that seem to fall under this umbrella but that were not labeled by the researchers as components of approaches to learning. These have included constructs such as academic intrinsic motivation, curiosity, engagement, executive function, focused attention, interest, preference for challenge, problem-solving flexibility, self-regulation, and task persistence.

Criteria for an Approaches-to-Learning Framework

If features from all of these sources were combined into a single, lengthy list, one would certainly gain a sense of the wide scope of the approaches-to-learning concept. However, such a laundry list would not be especially useful to teachers, other professionals, and policy makers. We need a framework that encompasses and organizes the essential components of approaches to learning. Such a framework should meet three criteria:

1. *Conceptually meaningful.* The framework should be organized in a way that makes sense from the perspective of developmental and educational theory and that is reasonably consistent with how others have organized this domain. This would allow those using the framework to align it with the work of others, making clear the connections and convergences.
2. *Evidence-based.* The framework should emphasize those approaches-to-learning components that appear most likely to be linked to important learning and developmental outcomes for children, as based on evidence from research and the professional practice.
3. *Practical.* The framework should have practical value for the day-to-day work of practitioners and policy makers. The framework should be understandable, easy to remember and describe, and applicable in a

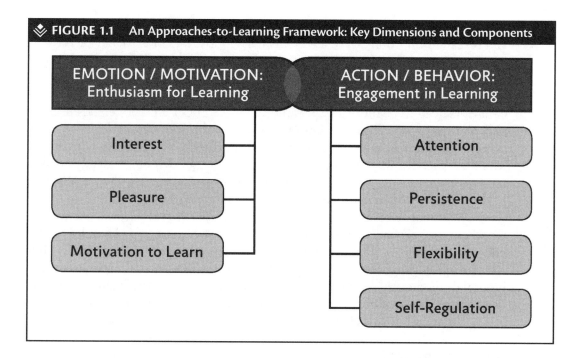

FIGURE 1.1   An Approaches-to-Learning Framework: Key Dimensions and Components

variety of contexts, focusing on those components that practitioners and policy makers can do something about.

The framework I suggest, visually summarized in Figure 1.1, is intended to meet these criteria.

ENTHUSIASM AND ENGAGEMENT: TWO PRIMARY DIMENSIONS OF POSITIVE APPROACHES TO LEARNING

The approaches-to-learning framework, which will be used throughout this book, is organized into two primary dimensions: *enthusiasm* and *engagement*, with each including a number of specific components. It is my strong belief that the concept of approaches to learning must include both feelings and actions—that is, both an emotional/motivational and an action/behavioral dimension. Although some might disagree with the exact terminology, this book will refer to the emotional/motivational dimension as "enthusiasm" and the action/behavioral dimension as "engagement."

Let's recall the description of 4-year-old Monica that opened this chapter. Undoubtedly, Monica is experiencing and showing positive approaches to learning—including both emotions and behaviors. Although her reserved temperament means that she shows her feelings in a low-key fashion, in her own way she can be said to be both enthusiastic and engaged.

Monica's example illustrates what has been found in much recent theory and research: Emotions serve as the primary motivators of all behavior (Hyson, 2004; Izard & Ackerman, 2000). Before Monica can exercise positive learning behaviors such as persistence or focused attention (as she did while dripping colored water onto the filter paper for 15 minutes without interruption), these behaviors need to be motivated by emotions—feelings such as interest, curiosity, and pleasure—as well as by impulses such as the motivation to learn or to become competent at something. And, of course, the relationship is two-way: Monica's successful, active engagement in the water-dripping activity further increases her feelings of pleasure, competence, and mastery—thus motivating her to get involved in and persist at other challenging projects.

Each of the two major dimensions—enthusiasm (the emotional/motivational dimension) and engagement (the behavioral dimension)—includes several components. These components seem to meet the criteria described earlier: They are conceptually meaningful, evidence-based, and practical. Later sections of this book will discuss these components in more detail; here I will simply explain their essentials and illustrate each with examples from the description of Monica at the beginning of this chapter.

Emotion/Motivation: Enthusiasm for Learning

As Figure 1.1 shows, I see enthusiasm for learning as including three components: *interest, pleasure,* and *motivation to learn.*

Interest. Young children seem to be born with keen interest and curiosity about the world around them. Theories and research in emotional development (Hyson, 2004; Izard & Ackerman, 2000) describe interest as one of the basic emotions. Feelings of interest are important in stimulating children's attention, exploration, and persistent behavior. Think about Monica: When she first sits down at the art table, the newness of the round pieces of filter paper, and the small droppers of colored water, are inviting and intriguing. Her face shows her interest—her eyes widen as she looks intently at the materials. For some children, this may be a passing interest, but Monica may be a child who, over time and with support, develops much deeper interests in these kinds of delicate, carefully wrought art activities, leading to further engagement and competence (Renninger, 2000; Renninger & Hidi, 2002). Like other components of approaches to learning, interest in learning must be respected and nurtured by early childhood educators.

Pleasure. Feelings of pleasure are also part of the emotional/motivational dimension of approaches to learning. Just as interest motivates children, pleasure (joy, happiness, enjoyment) can also be a powerful motivator of children's engagement in learning. As seen in Monica's extended work with the filter paper and colored water, children are likely to become deeply involved in activities that bring them pleasure. Monica's success in creating beautiful patterns brings her happiness, or "pleasure at being a cause," as Piaget (1962, p. 91) described it. These feelings will most likely motivate her to seek out similar activities in the future, creating a long-term positive learning spiral.

Motivation to learn. From infancy, children seem motivated to find out more about their world, to seek and master new challenges, and to become competent. This kind of motivation includes the desire to explore, control, and have effects on the environment, and a tendency to find learning new things a meaningful, worthwhile activity—even if the learning is not rewarded (Stipek, 2002).

Sitting alone at the art table, Monica does not need others' encouragement to continue with the sometimes-challenging task of creating complex patterns on the paper. No one has required her to participate in this activity; her involvement seems to be motivated simply by her desire to master a new challenge.

Action: Engagement in Learning

As seen in Figure 1.1, engagement in learning is the action-oriented dimension of approaches to learning. Although some apply a more specific meaning to the term engagement (e.g., McWilliam, Trivette, & Dunst, 1985), it can serve as a useful, easy-to-remember label for four components of this framework: *attention, persistence, flexibility,* and *self-regulation.*

Attention. Attention is a central component of engagement. As we will see in later chapters, focused attention is one of the mental processes that comprise the brain's critically important "executive function" (Rothbart, Sheese, & Posner, 2007; Zelazo, Müller, Frye, & Marcovitch, 2003). Monica maintains her focus for more than 15 minutes, able to shut out other noises nearby as she manipulates the paper and eyedroppers to create the effects she wants.

Persistence. Monica not only focuses her attention on the art activity, but she also persists or keeps trying even when the task is hard for her. Persistence when things are challenging also requires children to be able to tolerate frustration and to work through it to achieve a positive outcome—an important factor in school readiness (Fantuzzo et al., 2004).

Flexibility. Persistence is important, but persistence alone can cause children to become "stuck" using only one strategy (George & Greenfield, 2005). Monica and other children with positive approaches to learning have also developed flexible, innovative, and creative ways of handling challenges. Again, Monica gives us a good example. At first Monica squirted the water out of the eyedropper in one burst. The result did not seem pleasing, so the next time she tried a different tactic, applying tiny drops of water by squeezing the dropper slowly and rhythmically. Then she sat back, observed how that looked, and tried still another way of working.

Self-regulation. What is self-regulation? It can be described as children's "ability to act in a deliberate planned manner in governing much of their own behavior" (Bodrova & Leong, 2007, p. 127). One might see self-regulation as including some of the components we have listed above, but it seems to deserve separate emphasis in this framework. Self-regulation develops over time, and it needs much adult support, as we shall see in later chapters. Children who have developed appropriate self-regulation are able to guide their own physical actions, emotional expressions, and cognitive processes. Monica is able to manage her behavior, her feelings about the new art activity, and her thinking about what to do with the materials, with only a little adult guidance to get her started.

Why Call These "Positive" Approaches to Learning?

In this book, I frequently use the phrase "positive" approaches to learning to emphasize those emotions, motivations, and behaviors that are most likely to be connected to positive learning and developmental outcomes for children. Not all approaches to learning do produce good outcomes: children may approach learning tasks in ways that are distracted, disengaged, or discouraged—avoiding rather than eagerly encountering new challenges. It is easy to imagine another child in Monica's class sitting down at the art table, picking up a few pieces of filter paper, trying to manage the eyedropper, being unsuccessful at first, and quickly giving up, leaving the activity discouraged and frustrated. This pattern of behavior is also an "approach to learning," but it is not an approach that early childhood educators wish to strengthen.

USING THIS FRAMEWORK

These components of the approaches-to-learning framework do not form a complete description, but they seem especially important from the perspective of research and expert practice. They are described briefly here, in a sort of short-hand way, because that may make them easier to remember and apply.

This framework is intended to be used flexibly. Not a rigid instrument, it is the kind of tool that may help others organize their own thinking about children's approaches to learning. For example, the framework's two dimensions of enthusiasm and engagement may help practitioners be mindful that approaches to learning have both motivational and behavioral dimensions, so that they will nurture and connect both dimensions.

The framework can be used as a quick reminder of some key ideas, as a guide to planning curriculum and teaching strategies, as a way of organizing information from readings and professional development discussions, and as a communication tool with policy makers and other stakeholders. Finally, the framework is a work in progress: Its dimensions and components may indeed be reorganized, added to, or otherwise modified to better represent the realities of research and practice.

LOOKING BACK AND LOOKING FORWARD

Looking back at the descriptions of young children at the beginning of this chapter, it is probably now easier to see evidence of their enthusiasm and engagement, and of the specific components of these dimensions of approaches to learning. In the next chapter, I will describe why these characteristics are so important in children's development and learning.

 Reflection, Discussion, and Action

1. Review the descriptions of young children's behavior at the beginning of this chapter in light of the definitions and proposed components of approaches to learning. What evidence do you see in these descriptions of various components of positive approaches to learning? You might wish to begin collecting your own observational examples.

2. How would you describe to a group of families what you mean by "approaches to learning" in your own early childhood program? You might try to do this in two ways: orally, as in a presentation during a parent meeting, and in written form, as part of a parent handbook.

3. Review the specific components of approaches to learning as they are described in this chapter. From your personal or professional experience, is anything missing from this list? Which components do you think are the most important?

2 Why Do Positive Approaches to Learning Matter?

A small group of 3-year-olds are helping to paint a table. They are guided by their teacher but are using their own ideas about color and design. The colorfully decorated table and two chairs will be auctioned off at a school fundraising event the next weekend. One child, Ben, steps back and looks carefully at what has been done so far. Dipping his brush in a cup of purple paint, he tries to swirl it over a section of table leg that is still unpainted. Unable to reach the other side of the table leg, he peers under the table, squats, and reaches around to finish the job. Another child, Anna Maria, scrubs her brush intently and vigorously on one area of the table top, covering the last corner with bright blue paint. As she finishes, a big smile covers her face and she sighs with satisfaction.

YOU WILL RECALL that Chapter 1 defined the concept of young children's positive approaches to learning and introduced a framework for the major dimensions and components of approaches to learning. After reading that chapter, you can probably identify some of the dimensions and components of approaches to learning that are evident in Ben's and Anna Maria's work on the table-painting project.

But why should we care so much about this aspect of children's development and behavior? In this chapter I will summarize some persuasive evidence for why approaches to learning are so important—both for their intrinsic value and because they contribute to many aspects of children's lives. But I will also note that this evidence must be treated cautiously. The chapter will conclude by describing three ways to explain why approaches to learning are able to influence children's developmental and learning outcomes.

 Goals of This Chapter

After reading this chapter, you will be better able to

1. Convince others that everyone has the right to a childhood rich with experiences that support enthusiasm for and engagement in learning.

2. Convince others that children are likely to have better developmental and learning outcomes if their enthusiasm and engagement are intentionally strengthened.

3. Combine conviction with caution when applying the results of research on approaches to learning.

4. Explain how it is possible for young children's positive approaches to learning to have such broad and lasting effects.

ENTHUSIASM AND ENGAGEMENT HAVE INTRINSIC VALUE

The current educational climate has produced an almost exclusive focus on academic success. Therefore, much of the interest in approaches to learning has centered on their potential role in creating better achievement in later years of school. Although this chapter will describe much evidence of these kinds of results, it seems important to begin by celebrating the intrinsic value of qualities such as joy, pleasure, and deep engagement in learning.

Five-year-old Jessica, chin in hand, is gazing with fascination at the class pet, Fluffy the rabbit. For 10 minutes she sits with her friend Brandon, watching intently as Fluffy munches a carrot. The two children smile at each other from time to time, as they point at something that Fluffy is doing. Next, they start on their job for today—changing Fluffy's water. They patiently figure out how to maneuver the bottle out of the clip holding it to the cage, and they solve the problem of how to unscrew the bottle's cap, fill the bottle with water, and reinsert it into the cage. With happy expressions they sit in front of the cage again and watch Fluffy drinking the fresh water.

Is this experience important only because it will pay off in later academic and social-emotional competence? Certainly not. There is value in the sheer wonder of watching Fluffy eat his carrot and drink his water, and in the joyful satisfaction of solving a challenge with a friend.

This kind of deep absorption, which unites enthusiasm and engagement, has been called the experience of "flow." Csikszentmihalyi (1990) describes flow as the ultimate level of attention, absorption, and deep engagement in an activity, when "people are so attentive to the task at hand that they lose awareness of time and space" (National Research Council, 2003, p. 32). This description fits Jessica and Brandon's engagement as they seem to enter imaginatively into Fluffy's world, and into the task of getting fresh water for Fluffy, shutting out all the other activity in the room, even missing the call to begin cleaning up.

So before looking at the academic payoff for positive approaches to learning, we should remind ourselves that adults have the responsibility to ensure that childhood is joyful, wondrous, and rewarding in itself, not just as preparation for a successful future. Parents, teachers, and community members can create conditions that allow all children to experience these moments often and to develop interests that will be a rich, lasting source of enjoyment. It is simply a good thing for children to feel enthusiastic about learning, to be interested, curious, and happy as they learn, and to be deeply involved in new and challenging experiences.

ENTHUSIASM AND ENGAGEMENT FORM A FOUNDATION

Besides having intrinsic worth, positive approaches to learning produce other benefits for children. Ben and Anna Maria's careful absorption in painting the table, and Jessica and Brandon's joyful involvement in watching and caring for Fluffy, create a foundation for later positive outcomes. In this section I will summarize some of these benefits and will guide you toward resources that discuss this important research in greater depth, some of which will also be described in later chapters of this book. The benefits of positive approaches to learning appear most clearly in the cognitive and academic domains, but the benefits are seen in other areas that are also essential to children's development and learning. The evidence suggests that these are not simply short-term benefits, but that they extend across later years of education.

Benefits for Children's Academic and Cognitive Skills— Examples from Research

What are these benefits? Let's begin with research about the value of the overall approaches-to-learning umbrella for children's academic or cognitive outcomes, whether that umbrella is labeled "approaches to learning," "dispositions," "learning behaviors," "learning-related skills," or some other general term.

The largest study so far that examines the academic and cognitive benefits of children's approaches to learning is the Early Childhood Longitudinal Study conducted by the National Center for Education Statistics (NCES, 2002). In this study of a nationally representative sample of more than 20,000 children, those who were described by their teachers as having a more positive approach to learning when they started kindergarten (i.e., children who seemed more eager to learn, persisted at tasks, etc.) did better in reading and math in the spring of kindergarten and in first grade. In fact, they were more than twice as likely to score in the top 25% in reading and math as children who had less positive approaches to learning.

Similarly, in studying urban, low-income children in Head Start programs, John Fantuzzo and his colleagues have found that children who had more positive "learning behaviors" (characteristics such as focused attention, persistence, and initiative) developed stronger receptive and expressive vocabulary skills (Fantuzzo et al., 2004).

Another research team, Megan McClelland and her colleagues, has spent a number of years studying the influence of children's "learning-related skills" (including self-regulation and social competence) as the children move from kindergarten through sixth grade (McClelland et al., 2006). Even after controlling for factors such as IQ scores and mothers' education, children who had better learning-related skills in kindergarten had higher reading and math skills in the later grades.

These kinds of academic and cognitive benefits are also seen in studies that have focused on more specific dimensions and components of approaches to learning. Let's look first at some of the components of enthusiasm for learning, and then do the same with the dimension of engagement.

Interest. Interest, curiosity, inquisitiveness: Whatever this component is called, it does seem to predict academic and cognitive success. Much research shows that children's feelings of interest enhance their memory, comprehension, and selective attention (Renninger, Hidi, & Krapp, 1992). For example, because Jessica and Brandon are so interested in Fluffy (and in all animals), they remember numerous details about animal behavior and care. A meta-analysis integrating the results of many studies (Schiefele, Krapp, & Winteler, 1992) showed that interest is a consistent predictor of academic achievement. That is, those children who have stronger, deeper interest in specific areas are more likely to achieve well. And in a recent study by McTaggart, Frijters, and Barron (2005), kindergartners who said they have more interest in literacy had stronger word reading skills in second and third grade than less interested children.

Motivation to learn. Researchers find that children who have stronger motivation to learn are likely to develop higher levels of achievement. Turner and Johnson (2003) suggested how this might happen: By stimulating children to get more involved with things and people in their environment, this kind of motivation benefits children's longer term academic progress.

The terms that are used to describe this motivation vary (mastery motivation, motivation to learn, academic intrinsic motivation, intrinsic motivation, etc.), but the effects on academic and cognitive outcomes are quite consistent (Broussard & Garrison, 2004; Gottfried, 1990; Turner & Johnson, 2003). In the area of reading, for example, researchers found that children who are intrinsically motivated by a desire to be competent or to reach self-selected goals develop better comprehension skills than children who are motivated by external rewards (Guthrie & Alvermann, 1999). In another example, Turner and Johnson's (2003) study of 4-year-olds showed that differences in their mastery motivation (i.e., their motivation to solve problems in order to feel competent or to master a skill, without the need for external praise or rewards) predicted their later achievement in areas including expressive and receptive language; number, letter, and word identification; and counting, number concepts, and numerical problem-solving. When the researchers tried to predict children's later achievement from their scores on an academic skills pretest, those children with high mastery motivation were likely to end up achieving at a level considerably above what would have been expected from considering only their pretest scores. Again, motivation seemed to make the difference.

Engagement. School engagement is considered "a primary pathway by which motivational processes contribute to learning and development" (Hughes, Zhang, & Hill, 2006, p. 449). Much research shows that engagement—as seen in Jessica and Brandon's involvement in the job of helping Fluffy—is associated with positive academic and cognitive outcomes. Some of this research compares the academic and cognitive benefits of different "levels" of engagement, from very basic (e.g., just looking at objects) to higher or more sophisticated levels of engagement (e.g., more symbolic behavior, constructive play, and persistence). Not surprisingly, in these studies the children who showed higher levels of engagement turned out to be more competent and achieved more (Ridley, McWilliam, & Oates, 2000). And in their extensive study of children's transition from preschool to kindergarten, Rimm-Kaufman, La Paro, Downer, and Pianta (2005) found that academic success in kindergarten classrooms could be predicted from children's active engagement in classroom activities.

Self-regulation. In the framework for approaches to learning, I described self-regulation as a key component of engagement. Children who develop good self-regulatory abilities are more likely to be academically successful (Blair, 2002; Bodrova & Leong, 2007; Hyson, Copple, & Jones, 2006). Aspects of self-regulation include self-directed thinking and problem-solving, and metacognition (the ability to think about one's own thinking). One key feature of self-regulation is the ability to plan: Children who are able to plan, and carry out a plan, are more likely to develop more advanced cognitive skills (Hyson et al.,

2006). We saw examples of children's planning abilities as Anna Maria and Ben considered how to paint the table and then carried out their ideas. Jessica and Brandon, too, were using their planning skills when they worked out how to change the water in Fluffy's bottle.

Flexibility. Flexibility is another component of approaches to learning that has benefits for children's later achievement. Researchers have found that those children who were more flexible in their approach to problem-solving tasks—who were able to change their strategies as needed—had higher academic achievement later in kindergarten and even into the first grade (George & Greenfield, 2005). We saw this kind of flexibility when Brandon and Jessica did not get stuck on one way to get the water bottle out of the cage, but tried different strategies until they found one that worked. Similarly, Monica's flexible way of approaching the art activity in Chapter 1 would be likely to predict her achievement in academic or cognitive areas.

Social and Emotional Outcomes of Positive Approaches to Learning

Although much research has focused on the academic and cognitive benefits of positive approaches to learning, other benefits have been seen in the social and emotional areas. One would imagine, for example, that Ben would apply the same abilities to become deeply absorbed in an activity and to stick with a task that he demonstrated in the table painting project, when he became involved in pretend play with a group of children, or when he tried to make friends in a new first-grade class. A few examples of this line of research follow.

In the study of urban Head Start children described earlier, children who were rated more positively on their attention/persistence and on their attitude toward learning had more positive and constructive interactions when they played with other children, as observed by both parents and teachers (Fantuzzo et al., 2004). In the same study, children who were rated as having low levels of competence motivation were also more disconnected from other children during free play. Cybele Raver and her colleagues have shown how children's ability to regulate the way they express feelings such as anger or sadness predicts their later social competence as they interact with peers (Raver, Blackburn, Bancroft, & Torp, 1999).

WHY WOULD YOU EXPECT ACADEMIC AND SOCIAL BENEFITS?

Although research gaps still need to be filled in, and Figure 2.1 reminds us that caution is needed when interpreting the research that has been done, there are compelling reasons to believe that children's positive approaches to learning make uniquely important contributions to their development and learning. But *why?* Why would you expect that positive approaches to learning predict better

---

❧ FIGURE 2.1   Cautions About the Evidence

The evidence of benefits for positive approaches to learning is persuasive. But one should also be cautious in interpreting and using these studies.

+ There are gaps in the research. Not all aspects of approaches to learning have yet been studied to see what might be their connection to later academic, cognitive, and social competence.
+ Even when certain components have been studied, they may still need more precise definition and measurement. For example, few studies directly observe children's approaches to learning, relying instead on teachers' reports (though these can be informative).
+ Some of the most intriguing patterns of benefits have been found in research with elementary and secondary school students. Some, but not all, of these results may be applicable to younger children.
+ With some exceptions, research has been done with European American, middle-class children. As will be discussed later in this book, the pattern of benefits may differ for children from various cultural, linguistic, and income groups.
+ With the exception of work on engagement, children with disabilities have rarely been included in research on the benefits of positive approaches to learning.
+ Although higher levels of engagement, interest, persistence, and so on may statistically predict better educational and developmental outcomes, one cannot say with certainty that positive approaches to learning "cause" better outcomes. In some cases, the direction of influence may run the other way: For example, children who already have good academic skills might become more interested in learning as a result of having those skills.
+ A final caution: The kinds of predictions summarized here cannot say anything definite about individual children. Just because, in general, children who have lower levels of engagement, or who show less interest, have lower academic achievement in later grades does not mean that this will be the outcome in the case of one child. Nevertheless, these general patterns can help teachers identify children who may be at increased risk for later negative outcomes and who may benefit from well-planned interventions.

---

academic and social skills? Why would you expect that Anna Maria, who is so interested and persistent as she paints a table in her preschool, or Brandon, who is so motivated to learn everything he can about rabbits, would have better academic skills later on? Or that Anna Maria and Brandon would also be children who are accepted by others and can play constructively with them? There is nothing magical about positive approaches to learning, but clearly enthusiasm and engagement play a unique role in later learning and development.

Positive approaches to learning probably create these benefits in at least three ways: as keystone variables, as protective factors, and as contributors to

---

❖ **FIGURE 2.2   The Value of Positive Approaches to Learning**

In their effects on children's development and learning, positive approaches to learning—enthusiasm and engagement—create benefits in three ways:

◆ As *keystone variables*, which support achievement in other areas. If we strengthen children's enthusiasm and engagement, other areas will also be strengthened.

◆ As *protective factors*, which buffer or protect vulnerable children from a variety of risks to their development.

◆ As *contributors to positive cycles*, because young children with positive approaches to learning are viewed more positively by other people. Since these people may be able to provide enhanced learning opportunities, children have ever-growing chances to be involved in learning.

---

positive cycles. Figure 2.2 summarizes each of these, and we will take a closer look at them now.

Approaches to Learning as Keystone Variables

Just as a keystone in an arch over a doorway supports the entire stone structure, approaches to learning play a key role in supporting or keeping in place many other pieces of the school readiness structure. For example, "persistence and flexibility . . . are component skills that are important for learning in *all* school readiness domains" (George & Greenfield, 2005, p. 70; italics added). If Ben's flexibility in solving problems continues to be an important part of his approach to learning, this will have benefits in many areas—as he tries to figure out new words in a book, as he learns many ways to combine objects to make a set of 10, or as he tries several strategies in a third-grade science project. Such skills function as keystone variables (Barnett, Bauer, Ehrhardt, Lentz, & Stollar, 1996) not only because they can support achievement and success in a specific context but also because if we can strengthen these skills, we will simultaneously strengthen children's capacities in many other areas as well.

Approaches to Learning as Protective Factors for Children at Risk

Unfortunately, many children have conditions in their lives that increase the likelihood of negative outcomes for their development and learning. These may include factors such as poverty, living in dangerous neighborhoods, family violence, abuse or neglect, and risks from specific disabilities.

However, some children who experience serious, multiple risk factors develop well. Why is that? Researchers often find what they call "protective factors" in those children's lives. These factors, present within individual children or within families or communities, appear to buffer or protect those children from the negative effects of risk factors. In a sense, they increase children's resistance to risk and fortify children against developing negative outcomes.

More specifically, children's positive approaches to learning may serve as protective factors against a variety of negative outcomes. McWayne, Fantuzzo, and McDermott (2004) summarized studies showing that learning behaviors "have a protective influence against serious academic failure and maladjustment in school-age children" (p. 642). In high school, school engagement also serves as a protective factor for those students at greatest risk for dropping out (National Research Council, 2003).

Approaches to Learning as Jump-Starters of Positive Cycles

Education research has described a kind of "rich-get-richer and poor-get-poorer" phenomenon: Children who start school with more skills and abilities get even more over time, and the reverse is also true. Children who begin with low levels of skills often have less access to experiences and resources, thus lowering their achievement even more and further widening the gap. These cycles help explain the cumulative effects—over time—of children's positive approaches to learning. Enthusiastic and engaged children get more positive responses from their teachers, parents, and others; in turn, such responses increase the learning opportunities available to those children (de Kruif, McWilliam, Ridley, & Wakely, 2000; Rimm-Kaufman et al., 2005). One can imagine that a teacher would pay attention to Jessica's and Brandon's deep engagement with the class pet, would perhaps find some books about rabbits for them to look at, and in general would create pathways to new learning.

As this cycle continues, children who have positive approaches to learning are likely to learn more and become even more enthusiastic and engaged. For example, a child who greets a new learning task with high enthusiasm and engagement will probably stick with the task longer, learn more, and experience more success—thus leading to continued greater involvement in learning, more support from adults, and increased achievement. Research on children's interests (Renninger, 2000) shows that over time many children develop deeper and more focused interests—interests that play a key motivational role in their later learning, not just predicting better achievement but guiding them to more complex and rewarding learning opportunities. In the area of reading, children who have higher motivation to read usually spend more time engaged in reading, which leads to their choosing more challenging reading material, developing better reading comprehension, and experiencing greater self-efficacy as a reader (Guthrie & Wigfield, 2000).

Unfortunately, just as this cycle continues positively for some children, it takes the opposite course for others. Children who have poor reading skills in the early grades read less, and thus develop fewer skills and a smaller fund of background knowledge. Without such resources, the gap between these and other children keeps getting wider. Over time, these children may keep falling behind in school and ultimately are more likely to drop out than the children who are better readers (Guthrie & Wigfield, 2000). The same kind of negative cycle can be seen in young children who have little motivation to learn or who are already defeated and disengaged in their early years. These negative approaches to learning can start children on a downward trajectory that may seriously limit their later learning opportunities and achievements (Furrer & Skinner, 2003; Wigfield & Eccles, 2002; Wigfield & Tonks, 2004).

LOOKING BACK AND LOOKING FORWARD

Looking back at the 3-year-old table painters Ben and Anna Maria with this research in hand, there can be no doubt that we should care deeply about their interest, persistence, engagement, and ability to regulate their feelings and behavior. But an important question arises from looking at these children and others described in this chapter. Why is it that some children develop positive approaches to learning and others do not? Are they just born that way? Or are there other explanations—explanations that have great significance for how we teach young children? The next chapter will take up these questions.

 Reflection, Discussion, and Action

1. Looking back at your own childhood, can you see the effect of some positive approaches to learning on your later development and learning? In which area can you see this most clearly?

2. Share with others a memory of being in a state of "flow" either as a child or as an adult—when you were completely captured and engaged in an activity, almost unaware of space and time. What has been the effect of these experiences, and who or what helped make them possible?

3. Plan and, if possible, implement a short presentation for families or fellow educators about the importance of positive approaches to learning. Use the research described in this chapter, but be sure to tailor the presentation to your audience. An alternative might be to develop a handout or brochure that makes the same points.

How Do Children Develop
Positive Approaches to Learning?

Today, the children in this Head Start class are doing something different. Velma, the group's new assistant teacher, has planned an activity in which each child will make his or her own playdough. To introduce the activity, she uses the morning group time to show the children each of the ingredients as well as a finished ball of playdough.

After this introduction, the children all go to one long table, where each child has been given a small pile of flour. Velma pours some salt onto each child's pile and leaves the container on the table. Despite the teachers' reminders not to touch the flour yet, some children poke it with their fingers, while a few children blow at it vigorously. Sam stands quietly with his hands at his sides, looking down at the materials.

Velma tells the children to make a little hole with their fingers, so that she can add a bit of water and oil to each child's pile of flour and salt. Next, the children are to use their hands to mix the dough. Each child seems to have her or his own way of doing this: Claudia gets some flour on her patent leather shoes and looks down, worried, while Luz jumps right in but then makes a face and wipes her hands dramatically on a towel, laughing with the *other girls at her end of the table when her hands get too sticky to suit her. Ricardo is completely absorbed in the feel of the dough, rubbing it between his fingers and trying out the different textures as he mixes it. As he does this, he spies the container of salt on the table and surreptitiously dumps a large quantity onto his dough.*

Some of the children seem deeply engaged in trying to mix the ingredients, squeezing, flattening, and pulling bits of unmixed flour into their ball of dough. Other children lose interest or give up quickly, and still others are almost giddy with the excitement of these new materials. Some, like Sam, take a long time to become involved; yet once Sam begins, he coils his small ball of playdough into delicate, imaginative shapes. Gradually most of the children focus on the dough-mixing process as they begin to see results.

CHILDREN ARE BORN with an innate urge to connect with the people and things in the world. Unless they have significant disabilities or are living in desperate circumstances, babies are constantly touching, tasting, reaching, babbling—enthusiastic and engaged! But many things influence how those approaches to learning may develop in future months and years. As the children participate in Velma's playdough-making activity, multiple factors invisibly surround each child and the class as a whole, affecting how each child develops enthusiasm and engagement in learning. This chapter is about those factors—those "circles of influence."

Using Bronfenbrenner's ecological perspective on development as a framework, I will describe these intersecting circles of influence on children's approaches to learning, beginning with each child's individual and developmental characteristics, and then moving outward to the family, community, school, and culture. The chapter will also briefly describe policy and political environments as another set of influences on children's approaches to learning.

Before beginning this discussion, I should raise a few cautions. First, the examples in this chapter are just that—examples. They are not intended to describe exhaustively every possible influence on children's positive approaches to learning. You may think of or may have experienced even more. Second, as was emphasized in Chapter 2, the results of research apply only to large groups of children. General patterns may not apply to *specific* children, schools, or families. Third, we cannot "connect the dots" between any potential influence and any particular approach to learning in a simple cause–effect way. And, finally, children also influence their own development—the path of development is two-way. For example, although Velma's way of communicating with the children influences their behavior, at the same time the children's reactions also influence the way she responds to them.

Goals of This Chapter

After reading this chapter, you will be better able to

1. Look at children's approaches to learning with appreciation of their many possible and interacting influences.

2. Explain to others why it is important to be cautious about saying that certain approaches to learning are "caused by" certain influences.

3. Recognize how early childhood educators may be able to tap into each of these areas to positively affect children's approaches to learning.

WHAT INFLUENCES CHILDREN'S APPROACHES TO LEARNING? AN ECOLOGICAL PERSPECTIVE

Urie Bronfenbrenner's ecological perspective on human development may help organize an overview of the many intersecting influences on children's approaches to learning (Bronfenbrenner, 2000; Bronfenbrenner & Morris, 2006). Bronfenbrenner's theory emphasizes that, although every child brings certain "givens" into the world, he or she is constantly participating in many settings and systems, not only being affected by but also affecting those settings and systems. The children who are busy making playdough are no exception. Certainly, the experiences and interactions children have in their immediate environment are the most important contributors to their development. For each young child, the most influential experiences take place within the family and within the family's cultural practices. However, the child's experiences most likely also include early care and education programs, health care settings, and other community settings.

As Bronfenbrenner's theory further emphasizes, members of those settings also connect with and influence one another. For example, teachers, families, and health care providers may communicate regularly about a child's chronic illness. Further removed from the child's daily life, but also important in influencing her or his development, are settings and contexts such as the parents' workplace (e.g., does Luz's mother's employer make it possible for her to spend time at her child's school?). The outermost "circle" includes broad influences such as cultural values, customs, and public policies, which affect in many, sometimes indirect, ways how children are treated and what is expected of them in every setting. We will see specific examples of each of these as we take a closer look at the circles of influence, represented in Figure 3.1.

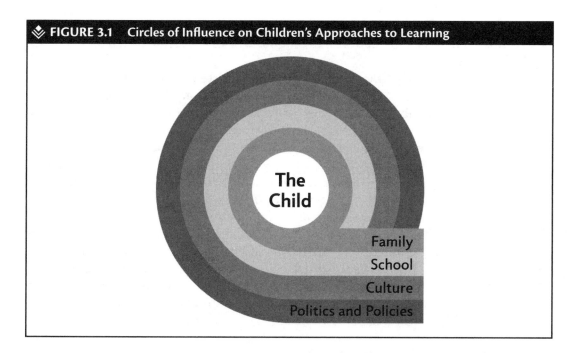

FIGURE 3.1   Circles of Influence on Children's Approaches to Learning

INDIVIDUAL DIFFERENCES IN CHILDREN'S CHARACTERISTICS

"They're just born that way"—or are they? There's no doubt that Sam, Ricardo, and Luz have each had a unique Sam-ness, Ricardo-ness, and Luz-ness since they were born. Sam's parents and grandparents say that they've noticed his cautious way of encountering new experiences since he was a baby. But does that mean that everything about Sam's approaches to learning was determined at birth? Not at all. When we take a closer look, in this chapter and later in the book, we will see that many factors influence the directions in which these seemingly fixed characteristics develop.

Temperament, Learning Styles, and Multiple Intelligences

Like other children, Sam has a distinctive, individual pattern of behaving and interacting with this world. In his case, it expresses itself in a cautious, somewhat fearful approach to new experiences (as we saw when he held back from even touching his playdough ingredients), combined with lots of persistence, even to the point of stubbornness, after he gets acquainted with a new experience. Just as children are born with their own eye color, body type, and so on, they come into the world with distinctive behavioral styles—individual patterns of behavior that are probably genetically influenced and that tend to persist over time (Rothbart & Bates, 2006).

These characteristics include differences in children's levels of distractibility, approach/withdrawal from new situations, adaptability, intensity, persistence, and attention span. When Sam grows up, it's more likely than not that he will approach his first job in the same cautious way that he approached his first week in Head Start.

Besides temperament, much has been written about children's so-called "cognitive styles" or "learning styles" (Rider, 1997). Some of this research suggests children have inborn preferences for processing information in either a visual, auditory, or physical way. Observing Ricardo's deep sensory absorption in mixing and manipulating the dough, one might see him as having a strong physical or "kinesthetic" learning style.

Similarly, Howard Gardner's (1993) theory of multiple intelligences describes seven primary types of intelligence. According to Gardner, individual children show early and persistent differences in their strengths in each area, resulting in a unique profile for each child. For example, the profile of social, active Luz might include strong emphasis on "interpersonal intelligence" and "bodily/kinesthetic intelligence," while Sam's strengths might be in the area of "spatial intelligence." Whether described as temperament, learning styles, or multiple intelligences, these kinds of differences may form the early roots of children's distinctive approaches to learning.

Girls, Boys, and Approaches to Learning

Does the fact that a child is a girl or a boy have some influence on her or his approaches to learning? Looking at the children making playdough, on average the girls appeared more planful and persistent than the boys—more self-regulated, if you will. Many of the girls approached the dough-making task in a focused, systematic way. And the only children who blew on the flour, dumped salt out of the container, or intentionally plopped a ball of dough onto the rug were boys.

Generally speaking, research confirms these impressions. Prekindergarten and kindergarten girls are apt to be more attentive and persistent as they work on learning tasks, whereas boys are likely to be more distractible and disruptive (McWayne et al., 2004). Teachers are apt to view boys, especially boys living in poverty, as especially distractible and hard to teach (Childs & McKay, 2001). And girls' greater attentiveness and persistence seems to explain some of their commonly observed superiority to boys in kindergarten literacy achievement (Ready, LoGerfo, Burkam, & Lee, 2005).

Inborn, Maybe, but Not Set in Stone

So some tendencies and behaviors related to children's approaches to learning seem to be inborn. However, these tendencies are not set in stone, and that is good news for early childhood educators and families. Even something like temperament (Rothbart & Bates, 2006), which is thought to be essentially "wired in," shows itself and develops differently depending on the extent to which people in a child's environment encourage its expression. Depending on the fit of their own temperament with that of a child, parents and teachers may try to change certain aspects of a child's temperament. For example, even if Sam tends to be reluctant to try new things, if Sam's parents and teachers encourage a bit more risk-taking, he may well shift his typical style to some extent, though he may never be a daring experimenter like his classmate Ricardo.

Many people have pointed out that children can develop strengths that go beyond their preferred learning style or innate abilities. While respecting children's early and persistent individual differences, educators can intentionally provide experiences to broaden children's repertoire of effective learning behaviors.

The same point can be made with respect to gender. Although the research shows some gender differences in children's approaches to learning, good early childhood programs can create opportunities for all children—boys and girls—to strengthen their persistence, flexibility, intrinsic motivation, and every other component of positive approaches to learning.

However, while acknowledging and respecting all of these individual differences, a major theme of this book is that children are not simply born with positive or negative approaches to learning. Labels like "Joachim is just not an attentive child," or "Kaeylin is basically unenthusiastic" will limit rather than expand children's capacities.

APPROACHES TO LEARNING GROW UP: THE INFLUENCE OF DEVELOPMENT

Having seen that the first "circle of influence" includes all of the innate characteristics that children bring into the world, let's look now at examples of the important developmental changes in children's approaches to learning from birth through the early grades of school. The Head Start children in our example are 4 years old or have just turned 5. If we had visited them the year before, would we have seen them express their enthusiasm and engagement in the same ways? To some extent, yes: Sam as a 3-year-old was probably hesitant yet also creative, and Luz would have most likely been impulsive and exuberantly sociable. But in the past year, major changes in the children's physical, cognitive, social, emotional, and language development have created new opportunities (and sometimes new challenges) in using those key approaches to learning.

Theoretical Perspectives

Why is this? Developmental theorists and researchers have described some of the pathways, trajectories, or sequences in which aspects of children's approaches to learning may develop—too many, in fact, to discuss in this chapter. Below are just a few illustrative examples; for more detail, Appendix A provides a chart summarizing some of these developmental sequences.

Some theories of child development offer insight into how approaches to learning may develop, even though none of these theories specifically uses the term approaches to learning in describing these behaviors. For example, the descriptions of typical developmental crises at each stage of Erikson's (1950) theory could be considered in terms of the different ways that children might approach learning tasks. In the preschool years, Erikson describes children as struggling with issues of initiative, approaching tasks with great bursts of bold energy and intrusiveness. These behaviors seem typical of at least some of the 4-year-olds in their first encounter with making playdough. Erikson's theory predicts that in a few years these children would approach such a task quite differently, when their central developmental crisis will revolve around issues of "industry versus inferiority." At that point, children might typically be concerned about the right way to make the playdough, thinking in terms of what bakers or sculptors might do and comparing their product with a culturally relevant standard.

Similarly, Vygotsky's theory describes sequences in the development of self-regulation, a central component of what we are calling the approaches-to-learning dimension of engagement. Developmentally, this group of 4-year-olds is becoming better able to act in a "deliberate, planned manner" (Bodrova & Leong, 2007, p. 127), but for now, many children in the class are still in a more reactive mode, impulsively responding to their feelings and their immediate environment. When Ricardo sees the big container of salt, for example, he grabs it and dumps it without being able to stop himself from acting on his impulse. Although Ricardo's impulsiveness may be an extreme example, most of the children in this class are still having great difficulty regulating their own behavior when faced with such a new, entrancing, and potentially messy stimulus!

Research in Neuroscience and Cognitive Development

New research in brain development offers additional insights into the development of approaches to learning. Neuroscientists would emphasize that maturation of the brain is one key factor, allowing older children to regulate their own behavior to a much greater extent than when they were younger. Furthermore, researchers see important developments in early childhood in those aspects of the brain's workings that are called "executive function," the ability to deal with problems (such as turning a pile of flour into a ball of playdough) in a deliberate yet flexible way (Rothbart et al., 2007; Zelazo et al., 2003). To do this, the brain needs to coordinate a number of mental processes; these include organizing, focusing attention, sustaining effort, monitoring, and self-regulating. These cognitive processes are similar to, and may be important underpinnings of, children's approaches to learning.

The Development of Specific Components

Beyond brain development, other researchers have tracked the very early development of some specific components of approaches to learning—again, without necessarily using that term. For example, Barrett, Morgan, and Maslin-Cole (1993) described stages in development of children's "mastery motivation," from birth to age 3: First, babies try to control events or toys; then they try to meet some standards (what the researchers call "task-related mastery"); and finally, toddlers evaluate themselves based on comparing their own performance with some specific standards.

Researchers have also traced the development of achievement motivation in children (this work is well summarized in Wigfield, Eccles, Schiefele, Roeser, & Davis-Kean, 2006). For instance, children as young as 2½ react to failure by showing negative emotion or avoiding looking at adults. Researchers also find developmental changes in how children interpret their failure. Very young children, under age 2, are not concerned about what others think of their performance; next, children begin to care what adults think; and as they get older, they become able to evaluate their own success or failure. Yet even in preschool there are individual differences, with some 4- and 5-year-olds reacting very negatively to failure on learning tasks.

Children with Disabilities

As we think about the development of children's approaches to learning over the early childhood years, it is important to keep in mind that this pathway may be different for children who have developmental delays or disabilities. For a child with a disability, certain components of approaches to learning may take longer to develop, or the child may show enthusiasm or engagement with behaviors different from those of a typically developing child. For example, one of the children making playdough is Teresa, who has Down syndrome. Although she is the same chronological age as her classmates, Teresa's developmental age limits her current ability to sustain engagement in the playdough-making task (de Kruif & McWilliam, 1999). Another child in the class, Raymond, has been diagnosed with autism; this disability creates challenges in his ability to use flexible problem-solving strategies. For example, Raymond does not change his technique for mixing the dough even when that strategy does not lead to success, and he does not turn to other children for ideas or help in solving the challenge of how to mix the dough.

However, one cannot generalize about children with disabilities. First, each child who has a disability is also an individual, with the individual quirks and characteristics that all children have. Teresa's neighbor Brock also has Down syndrome, but he has a very different style of behavior than Teresa, although both have the same disability and are the same age. Second, different disabilities may have different implications for the development of positive approaches to learning. Zachary has mild cerebral palsy, but the disability has not affected Zachary's development of any aspects of positive approaches to learning. His only difficulty is that other children and adults sometimes do not understand his words when he tries to express his enthusiasm or desire for engagement in a task. Like Zachary, Brock, Raymond, and Teresa, *all* children have potential to develop positive approaches to learning, though perhaps on different timetables and in different ways.

FAMILY INFLUENCES

Children are not just individuals but are members of families and communities. Chapter 9 will recommend ways in which early childhood programs may partner with families to support children's positive approaches to learning. This chapter simply describes some of the ways in which families make a difference.

A major influence on approaches to learning is the quality of a child's relationship with her or his family. Children with secure attachment relationships are likely to develop more persistent, enthusiastic, and curious ways of approaching problem-solving tasks, from the toddler years into preschool and kindergarten (Arend, Gove, & Sroufe, 1979; Waters, Wippman, & Sroufe, 1979). These relationships might explain at least some of the individual differences in the Head Start children's reactions to the new experience of making their own playdough. More generally, children who have strong "relatedness" to their parents "may enter the classroom with . . . a willing attitude and the desire to concentrate on the classroom agenda" (Furrer & Skinner, 2003, p. 159). Furrer and Skinner, along with Howes and Ritchie (2002), have also found that children who are closer to their parents may subsequently form closer relationships with their teachers—relationships that in turn influence their level of academic motivation and engagement.

Parents' own beliefs about learning, and the way they translate those beliefs into action, may also influence their children's approaches to learning. For example, research suggests that children whose parents encourage them to become involved in learning for its own sake (not just to receive rewards) have greater intrinsic motivation to learn (Gottfried, Fleming, & Gottfried, 1994).

THE INFLUENCE OF SCHOOL

At an early age, most children in the United States begin to spend time in out-of-home care and education programs. Whether it is a child care center, a family child care home, prekindergarten, a Head Start classroom, kindergarten, or the primary grades, "school" is an important circle of influence on young children's approaches to learning, both directly and indirectly (through the school's relationship with families). The potential sources of influence include children's relationships with their teachers, as well as the quality of the program, curriculum, and teaching practices.

Relationships with Teachers

Among the many benefits of children's positive relationships with their teachers (Pianta, 2000), a very important plus is the positive effect on children's motivation to learn. As Furrer and Skinner (2003) put it,

Feelings of relatedness tapped by measures of school climate and quality of teacher–student relationships, as well as feelings of belonging, inclusion, acceptance, importance, and interpersonal support, have been linked to important academic outcomes, including self-efficacy, success expectations, achievement values, positive affect, effort, engagement, interest in school, task goal orientation, and school marks. (p. 149)

Although Furrer and Skinner's statement is based on research with somewhat older children, it is likely that these positive connections between teacher–child relationships and children's motivation to learn begin much earlier. In a study of children's engagement in classroom activities in North Carolina child care centers, researchers from the Frank Porter Graham (FPG) Child Development Center (2001) found that in programs where the teachers were especially warm and sensitive, a higher percentage of children were observed to be actively engaged.

In the observation from which the chapter opening vignette was drawn, one could sense the children's happiness at Velma's warm involvement and attention. This warmth seemed to keep some of the more distractible boys focused on the activity, even though her way of organizing the activity showed her inexperience as an early childhood teacher.

In addition to benefiting from close relationships with teachers, children also model their own approaches to learning on those they see in their teachers. Teachers who themselves have more of a "mastery orientation" (learning to become more competent, rather than just to pass a test or get a reward) influence the children in their classrooms to be more mastery-oriented and to have more intrinsic motivation to learn (Midgley, 2002).

Other Aspects of Program Quality

Besides the influence of a teacher's relationship with children, other aspects of quality in early childhood education are able to influence children's positive approaches to learning. These range from overall program quality to more specific aspects of curriculum and teaching practices.

For example, in the FPG study, the researchers found that the level of program quality correlated with the extent and level of the children's engagement (FPG Child Development Center, 2001). Children in higher quality classrooms were more likely to be engaged in activities in a more sophisticated and focused way than children in programs rated as lower in quality. The effect of program quality on children's engagement was especially evident in classrooms that served toddlers rather than older preschoolers. As the researchers noted, it may be that in order for toddlers to become and remain engaged, they must have the sort of teacher support and scaffolding provided in higher quality classrooms.

Much research indicates that positive approaches to learning will be supported by an early childhood curriculum that fosters children's choice, independence, and planning, and that offers children activities with appropriate levels of challenge and complexity (Hyson et al., 2006; Stipek & Seal, 2001). As we will see in Chapter 6, a number of curricula have these characteristics. Similarly, Rimm-Kaufman et al. (2005) found that the way early childhood teachers organize the environment and interact with children makes a difference in children's involvement in learning. For example, children are more involved when teachers rely more on small groups and when they build or elaborate on children's own ideas.

Studies of older children, summarized in Midgley (2002), Wigfield and Eccles (2002), and Wigfield et al. (2006), have found that children's motivation to learn and their engagement in learning are supported by teaching practices that communicate clear expectations, encourage children's active involvement and collaboration, and give children helpful guidance without overcontrolling every aspect of children's actions.

CULTURAL INFLUENCES

The circles-of-influence image (Figure 3.1) places culture at quite a distance from the individual child. However, Bronfenbrenner and others have emphasized that culture's influence is pervasive, connecting with and permeating every other system that influences a child's development (Bronfenbrenner, 2000; Rogoff, 2003). This section suggests some of the many ways in which culture may influence young children's approaches to learning. Subsequent chapters will weave these cultural issues into discussions of relationships, curriculum, teaching practices, assessment, and family involvement, continually emphasizing that tools and strategies to support children's approaches to learning are never culture-free.

The group of children described in the opening vignette, like those in most other early childhood programs today, is culturally diverse. The bilingual Head Start program that the children attend is located in a community center in a low-income urban neighborhood. The neighborhood is predominantly Hispanic, including children whose families have immigrated more or less recently and who came from many different countries, each with its own traditions and values. The program also enrolls a number of African American children and a few who are White or Asian.

Little research has examined cultural influences on specific aspects of children's approaches to learning. Studies of how children develop their motivation to learn have primarily been conducted with White, middle-class children. But many researchers, though not focusing specifically on approaches to learning, have studied broader cultural influences on children's development (Rogoff, 2003; Schweder et al., 2006). Their insights may indirectly help us understand how linguistic and cultural diversity may affect children's enthusiasm and engagement.

Whatever their culture, all children probably share certain essentials that we are calling positive approaches to learning. Enthusiasm is evident in all children; children in every culture can be interested, joyful, and motivated to learn. Engagement is also part of all children's behavioral repertoire; children in every culture can be attentive, persistent, flexible, and self-regulated. But within these essentials, culture still remains a powerful influence on how children's approaches to learning develop and are expressed in their behavior. Let's look at a few examples.

First, children growing up in different cultures may vary in how persistent, attentive, or self-regulated they seem to be. For example, Blinco (1992) found that on the average, Japanese first-graders were significantly more persistent in completing tasks than their U.S. counterparts. The most likely explanation is that broad cultural values influence how much families may encourage their children's persistence. For many U.S. families, persistence may not be an important value, at least for younger children.

Most descriptions of approaches to learning focus on children's *individual* feelings and behaviors—the child's own attention, persistence, engagement, motivation, and so on. Yet the United States is in the minority in its dominant cultural emphasis on individualism and independence. Seventy percent of the world's cultures have a more collaborative, interdependent orientation than is found in the dominant U.S. culture. In these cultures, group efforts are valued and encouraged far more than the efforts made by individuals (Gutiérrez & Rogoff, 2003; Rogoff, 2003).

Many of the culturally diverse children enrolled in U.S. early childhood programs may have been encouraged to adopt those collaborative values by their families and community. Although this point has often been made about children from non-U.S. cultures, Ladson-Billings (1995, 1997) and others have noted the same orientation toward cooperative approaches to learning among many African American students, as well as among American Indian and Alaska Native children (Pewewardy & Hammer, 2003).

Culture also influences children's responses to various kinds of learning tasks and experiences. We know that children tend to be more motivated to engage in tasks that are optimally challenging—neither too far above nor too far below their capacities. But this match depends greatly on what the child's cultural environment considers challenging, and what experiences the child has had within that culture. What is an interesting challenge within one culture may be routine within another. In the playdough-making activity, some of the children were frustrated at first when they tried to combine the ingredients, apparently having had few experiences with this process. In contrast, many of the Hispanic children in the class help their mothers and grandmothers make tortillas every day. Mixing, slapping, and stretching the dough were second nature for these children; using these skills in a new activity created much enjoyment and engagement.

Culture also influences how children display their approaches to learning. Some cultures value and encourage vivid expressions of emotion; in other cultures, children may be less expressive in showing their interest and joy, though their underlying feelings may be the same (Hyson, 2004). Similarly, when children focus their attention on a learning task, culture may influence whether they show this attention in intense gazes or in sidelong glances, and whether children explore the learning material physically or simply watch others demonstrate the activity (Rogoff, 2003).

A final example: Children's culture may also influence how they respond to the other circles of influence as they develop positive approaches to learning. In an earlier section of this chapter, we saw that positive approaches to learning are enhanced when children have warm relationships with their teachers. This is true for all children but seems especially important for ethnic minority students, who tend to flourish when teachers combine warm, personal relationships with high expectations (Brophy, 2004; Delpit, 2006).

This discussion of cultural influences should end by emphasizing that children's culture is a great potential asset to their approaches to learning. As we will see in later chapters, culturally responsive teaching increases the chances that all children, whatever their culture, language, and ethnicity, will develop enthusiasm and engagement—perhaps stimulated by different things and expressed in different ways, but always benefiting their development and learning.

POLITICAL AND POLICY INFLUENCES

Unlike their experience of culture, children do not seem to experience the influence of politics and public policies on a daily basis—yet this circle of influence is, in its own way, as pervasive as that of culture. What are the ways in which the political and public policy context can influence children's approaches to learning? Below we will look briefly at some potentially positive effects. However, because recent policy trends have created significant risks to children's enthusiasm and engagement, much of the policy discussion will occur in the next chapter, where the focus is on factors that undermine children's approaches to learning.

As described in Chapter 1, the National Education Goals Panel brought the concept of approaches to learning into public awareness as part of its focus on school readiness. More recently, states have been developing Early Learning Standards. Some states have specifically included approaches to learning as a separate standards category or have embedded some of the dimensions and components in other standards categories, such as "Social-Emotional Development" (Scott-Little et al., 2005). Similarly, when the Head Start Bureau (2001) developed its Child Outcomes Framework, it decided to include approaches to learning as a distinct category. When policy makers have engaged in these kinds of actions, greater attention has been placed on enthusiasm and engagement as key dimensions of children's development and as key dimensions for early childhood educators to emphasize.

LOOKING BACK AND LOOKING FORWARD

This chapter has described the many interlocking circles of influence that can produce positive approaches to learning for young children. As we have seen, children come into the world with some basic behavior patterns or temperament/

learning style characteristics. Some children may also come into the world with disabilities or developmental delays. Yet these individual characteristics are only part of the picture. Complex influences, ranging from family to school to culture to public policies, work together to affect each child's enthusiasm for and engagement in learning.

As we trace these processes, we should also remember that early childhood professionals can positively affect children's approaches to learning by becoming involved in each of these circles of influence. For example, early childhood educators can align their classroom practices with families' cultural values; they can select curriculum that intentionally fosters interest, engagement, persistence, and other positive approaches to learning; they can work to understand and influence public policies that might promote attention to approaches to learning. Together, these and other actions may have substantial effects on children's enthusiasm and engagement, and ultimately on their development and learning.

This chapter has emphasized the positive, describing the many ways in which children's approaches to learning may be supported, nurtured, and shaped by the settings and systems that affect their lives. In contrast, the next chapter will uncover the factors that increasingly undermine the enthusiasm and engagement that early childhood educators wish to promote.

Reflection, Discussion, and Action

1. In your work with young children, where do you see the greatest potential for you to influence children's ability to develop positive approaches to learning? Is it at the classroom level, in the policy arena, with families, or some combination of these areas?

2. To explore the ideas in this chapter, you might focus on a child whom you have gotten to know well. In observing her or his behavior, think about not just the *what* but also the *why* of the child's approaches to learning. What are all of the possible circles of influence that may contribute to the child's particular patterns of enthusiasm and engagement? You might wish to select two children for purposes of comparison.

3. If you have not done so before, look at your own state's Early Learning Standards using this link: http://nccic.acf.hhs.gov/pubs/goodstart/elgwebsites.html. To what extent do you see approaches to learning represented, either as a distinct category or incorporated into other areas? Knowing more about the importance of this aspect of early development and learning, are you satisfied with how this domain has been represented?

What Undermines Children's Positive Approaches to Learning?

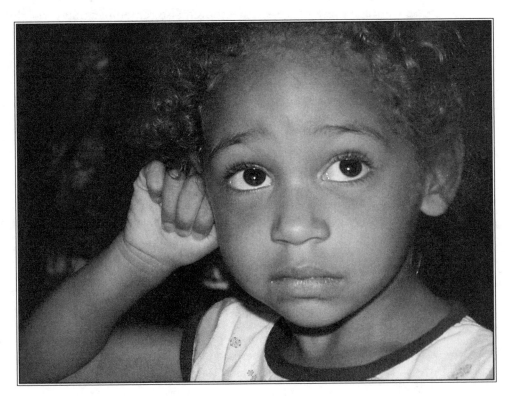

Ms. Manning's first-graders have gathered on the rug, where Ms. Manning is teaching a lesson about Christopher Columbus and the upcoming Columbus Day holiday. As she shows the children pictures from the district's social studies curriculum kit, she reads the information related to each picture. Some of the children are sitting cross-legged with their eyes on the pictures, but Rodney is staring off into the distance, and other children are twisting around to check some noise in the hall. Oscar has gotten up and wandered to the other side of the room; Ms Manning stops to bring him back to the circle. Ellie and Rachette begin pushing each other as they compete for the same space on the rug.

Ms. Manning asks the class questions to check their recall of the information she has given them; a few children raise their hands to answer. She reminds them that they will get extra play time if they pay attention and answer the questions. As the time passes, however, more and more children become disinterested and disruptive. Finally Ms. Manning dismisses them to tables, where they will practice writing the letter "M" on lined paper. Ms. Manning walks from one table to another. Oscar sits with his head on his arms, having tried one "M" without success. When his teacher asks why he is not doing what he's supposed to do, Oscar just shakes his head.

DID THE MORNING just get off to an especially bad start, or was more going on here? This classroom example is fictional, but the events are typical of an increasingly familiar pattern in early childhood education.

In previous chapters we have seen examples of children joyfully engaged in learning activities, seeking out, focusing on, and persisting at challenging tasks without coercion or rewards. I have summarized research about how these positive approaches to learning develop and about what may affect that development. We have seen that a number of influences can strengthen children's *enthusiasm*—their interest, pleasure, and motivation to learn—and their *engagement*—their attention, persistence, flexibility, and self-regulation.

But other influences can weaken or undermine these positive approaches to learning. In this chapter I will explain why teachers and others are so concerned about the number of children who lack positive approaches to learning. I will describe some influences that may contribute to these negative patterns, ranging from unsupportive relationships to public policies that may suppress the very enthusiasm and engagement that are keys to later academic success.

These influences have the potential to undermine *all* children's positive approaches to learning, but they may have especially negative effects on children who are already vulnerable because of poverty, disability, or other risk factors, as well as on children who are culturally and linguistically diverse.

 Goals of This Chapter

After reading this chapter, you will be better able to

1. Describe current concerns about, and evidence of, discouraged and disengaged approaches to learning among young children.

2. Identify some of the factors that may undermine children's positive approaches to learning.

3. Analyze these factors in light of situations in your own environment.

BECOMING DISCOURAGED AND DISENGAGED— THE DOWNWARD SPIRAL

Many experienced early childhood educators feel that today's children have less positive attitudes toward learning and less positive learning behaviors than these educators have seen in the past. Rather than being enthusiastic and engaged, many children, even in preschool, seem *un*enthusiastic and *dis*engaged, already discouraged and defeated by learning challenges. As compared with other children their age, they do not persist at difficult tasks and, like Oscar, may avoid those kinds of experiences altogether. They appear unable to plan ahead, and they tackle everyday problems in unsystematic ways. These children are unlikely to become involved in classroom activities; when they are involved, their level of engagement may remain superficial rather than becoming deeper and more complex. Some experienced teachers say that fewer children than in the past have intense individual interests in specific topics or activities, such as finding insects, learning about dinosaurs, building structures, or painting. Finally, these teachers say that many children exert effort only when they think they will be rewarded, or when they wish to avoid disapproval.

So it appears that many children begin their school years already discouraged and disengaged. When we consider that children's enthusiasm and engagement typically *decline* over the years that they are in school, there is indeed much cause for concern.

Specifically, researchers have found that as children move through elementary and middle school, they tend to become less confident about their own competence and less intrinsically motivated to learn, especially when it comes to academic subjects (Harter, 1996; National Research Council, 2003; Wigfield & Tonks, 2004). This downward trend is quite clear in children's intrinsic motivation to read—which, in turn, appears to influence children's engagement in reading, their reading comprehension, and their reading achievement (Guthrie & Wigfield, 2000).

WHAT MAY CONTRIBUTE TO CHILDREN'S NEGATIVE APPROACHES TO LEARNING?

As I emphasize throughout this book, children are enthusiastic and engaged, or discouraged and disengaged, not because they're just born that way, but because of many influences on their lives. Let's look at some of the factors that may contribute to negative patterns in children's approaches to learning, in early childhood and beyond. These are summarized in Figure 4.1 and discussed in detail in the next sections.

Unsupportive Relationships Between Adults and Children

Just as warm, supportive relationships encourage children's positive approaches to learning, the absence of such relationships serves to undermine them. Relationships cannot be built without interactions, and many children have limited opportunities to interact with their teachers. Classroom observations in the National Prekindergarten Study showed that, on average, children were directly involved with a teacher or other adult less than one third of the time (Clifford et al., 2005; Pianta et al., 2005).

When young children do interact with teachers, those interactions are not always positive. For example, teachers seldom talk about emotions with children (Hyson, 2003). A significant number of teachers are detached or harsh in their

---

❧ FIGURE 4.1   Factors That Undermine Young Children's Positive Approaches to Learning

These are some of the factors that can undermine young children's enthusiasm and engagement. To what extent do you see these in your own professional environment?

- ◆ Unsupportive relationships between adults and children
- ◆ Unchallenging, irrelevant curriculum
- ◆ Teaching methods that fail to support children's engagement and motivation to learn
- ◆ Rushed, rigid schedules
- ◆ Reliance on external rewards to promote achievement
- ◆ Policies related to standards for children's learning
- ◆ Policies related to high-stakes assessment

---

interactions with young children; these negative patterns are especially frequent in infant–toddler programs (Phillips & Adams, 2001). Such interactions are unlikely to produce secure, supportive relationships, as illustrated in Ms. Manning's distant and critical interactions with Oscar. And children who have insecure relationships with adults (parents or teachers) are often less enthusiastic and less persistent when they face challenging tasks (Arend et al., 1979; Howes & Ritchie, 2002).

It is hard to know whether young children today are less likely to have close relationships with their teachers than in the past. However, teachers from prekindergarten through the primary grades are feeling the pressures of meeting academic standards, "covering" a curriculum, and preparing for high-stakes testing. Taken together, these pressures may make it harder for teachers to build close relationships with individual children. If that indeed is the case, many children may not gain the security that those relationships provide—security that helps young children explore new learning opportunities, take risks in their learning, and tackle sometimes frustrating learning tasks.

Unchallenging, Irrelevant Curriculum

Children benefit when a program has a clearly articulated and intentionally implemented curriculum (Frede & Ackerman, 2007; Hyson, 2007). As Chapter 3 described, when children have the opportunity to get involved in complex, challenging, appropriate curriculum, they experience greater enthusiasm and engagement. In turn, these positive approaches to learning tend to produce higher achievement.

But much early childhood curriculum is not very engaging and not very effective. This sort of curriculum may be found at one of two unfavorable extremes. At one end is a shallow, perhaps "fun" curriculum that fails to respect children's intelligence. The other extreme is a curriculum that is so far beyond children's level of understanding and background knowledge that it results in frustration. Furthermore, a number of early childhood curricula emphasize isolated skills rather than embedding skill development within broader, more engaging content. Curriculum often fails to connect with or deepen young children's interests. Finally, curriculum may not be culturally responsive, further undermining the interest and engagement of diverse young children. Many of these problems are evident in the social studies curriculum used in Ms. Manning's class, which was described in the opening vignette. The curriculum seems to emphasize rote learning of isolated facts (in this case, about Christopher Columbus) and makes no effort to respond to children's interests, cultures, or abilities.

When early childhood curriculum has these kinds of problems, children's positive approaches to learning are likely to be undermined. Like the children in Ms. Manning's class, when faced with such a curriculum, young children often respond with inattention, negative behavior, and avoidance of learning tasks. Chapter 6 will suggest ways in which early childhood programs can avoid these negative consequences, drawing on curriculum models that are both cognitively challenging and engaging.

Teaching Methods That Undermine Engagement and Motivation

How children are taught is at least as important as *what* they are taught, when it comes to supporting or undermining positive approaches to learning. An ethnographic study of nine third-grade teachers identified 45 different teaching practices that promoted children's academic engagement and motivation, along with 19 practices that served to undermine children's motivation (Dolezal, Welsh, Pressley, & Vincent, 2003). Figure 4.2 lists and gives examples of some of these "undermining" practices, many of which may be seen in Ms. Manning's first-grade class.

Her instructional practices appear typical of what has been seen in large-scale research. The multistate National Prekindergarten Study (Clifford et al., 2005; Pianta et al., 2005) found that teachers spent a high proportion of their time simply managing routine activities (snack, lining up, etc.). When they were actually teaching, they used methods that were unlikely to create positive approaches to learning. Lengthy whole-group instruction dominated, and not surprisingly in these settings children were less interested and engaged. These patterns continue in later grades. In a follow-up to the National Institute of Child Health and Human Development's (NICHD) large-scale child care study, the NICHD Early Child Care Research Network (2005) found that third-grade teachers overwhelmingly used rote teaching strategies even when the lesson content might have suggested a different, higher level approach. Furthermore, teachers varied their methods very little during teaching activities. Probably as a result, although children often went along with what the teachers asked of them, the children showed low levels of enthusiasm and engagement.

> ### ☙ FIGURE 4.2   Examples of Teaching Practices That Undermine Children's Motivation to Learn
>
> The following examples are drawn from a study of teachers' efforts to motivate third-grade students (Dolezal et al., 2003). In this study, children's engagement varied dramatically depending on their teacher. Here are some of the strategies that were typical of teachers whose students showed very low levels of engagement—practices that appear to undermine children's motivation to learn. Following each strategy is an example that applies to early childhood programs.
>
> ◆ Emphasizing ability rather than effort
>
> *During a lesson, some children call out that they are stupid. The teacher does not stop these comments but says, "Let me have someone who is smart."*
>
> ◆ Emphasizing winning or being the best rather than working together
>
> *The teacher has a poetry contest; students hold up cards rating the poems other students read on a 1–4 scale.*
>
> ◆ Providing tasks that offer no challenge
>
> *The teacher gives cut-and-paste or workbook activities; some activities are fun but teach little to the children.*
>
> ◆ Failing to make connections between lessons and other concepts or experiences
>
> *Near Martin Luther King Day, the activities are almost entirely about George Washington.*
>
> ◆ Failing to provide help for children who are struggling to master a skill
>
> *The teacher says, "You are so lazy. Just look it up; it's simple."*

Rushed, Rigid Schedules

Children need time to build their engagement, persistence, and motivation to learn. "Best practice" guidelines in early childhood education typically recommend scheduling large blocks of time during the day when children can investigate phenomena, try out various problem-solving strategies, and deepen their involvement in a project or other learning task (Bredekamp & Copple, 1997). Those who discuss moving from half-day to full-day kindergarten have referred to the potential benefits of more leisurely scheduling than is possible in a half-day program (Elicker & Mathur, 1997; Fromberg, 1992). Such a predictable yet relaxed and open-ended framework may be especially helpful in accommodating children whose learning pace is different because of temperament, culture, or disabilities.

However, the schedules in many early childhood classrooms give children little opportunity to learn how to focus their attention, persist over time, engage more fully in learning experiences, or develop in-depth interest in a topic. Half-day kindergarten teachers often describe a schedule overload, in which they feel they are continually racing from one content area or special program to another. Some school districts, especially those with Reading First programs, have taken this a step further. They mandate exactly when each class and each teacher should be finished with a specific topic, unit, or area of instruction. These "pacing schedules" seem likely to pressure both teachers and children, working against the development of engagement and persistence and potentially undermining intrinsic motivation to learn.

Reliance on External Rewards to Motivate Achievement

As described in Chapter 1, an important component of positive approaches to learning is children's intrinsic motivation to learn. Both parents and teachers often assume that rewards are needed to create motivation and achievement. However, research suggests that children's intrinsic motivation may actually be undermined when adults rely too much on external rewards (Elliot & Dweck, 2005; Stipek, 2002).

Parents have the best intentions when they reward their children for becoming involved in learning activities. Some parents give their young children special treats or prizes for reading books or completing assignments. Although sometimes producing short-term compliance, these motivators may backfire in the longer run, as children become overly dependent on the rewards (Gottfried et al., 1994; Stipek & Seal, 2001).

Similar cautions have been expressed about the use of external rewards in school (Stipek, 2002; Wigfield et al., 2006), where such motivational strategies begin early and increase over the elementary and high school years. Across these years, external rewards, such as the extra play time Ms. Manning promises, are unlikely to promote intrinsic motivation to learn, or to foster real engagement in learning. For example, a major report on promoting high school students' engagement found that the use of rewards to motivate disengaged students (e.g., giving prizes for coming to school more often) usually resulted in superficial compliance (National Research Council, 2003). However, in the absence of other strategies to promote in-depth cognitive engagement, students ended up not learning any more. Their bodies may have been in school, but their minds remained elsewhere.

BEYOND SYMPTOMS TO UNDERLYING CAUSES

Faced with this array of negative influences, it is easy to blame teachers, schools, or children's parents. However, the surface symptoms may mask the underlying causes.

Policies Related to Standards for Children's Learning

Although public policies have the potential to support children's positive approaches to learning, some policies have created conditions that have had the opposite effect.

Every state has standards describing what K–12 students should know and be able to do, and now almost every state has developed "early learning guidelines" or standards for children below kindergarten age. There is nothing inherently wrong with standards; at their best, these standards can have beneficial results (NAEYC & National Association of Early Childhood Specialists in State Departments of Education [NAECS/SDE], 2002). However, the sheer number of items in many states' standards may lead to teaching practices that do not promote in-depth engagement and learning (Kendall & Marzano, 1995; Neuman & Roskos, 2005).

Faced with such overwhelming numbers of standards and benchmarks, teachers may feel the need to skim through the curriculum, as seemed to be happening in Ms. Manning's effort to "cover" Columbus and the Columbus Day holiday on a surface level. Although it is possible to prioritize and address large numbers of standards in a more in-depth, integrated fashion—emphasizing what have been called "power standards" (Reeves, 2002)—a lack of professional development and administrative support makes it hard for teachers to do this.

Some versions of the standards movement may contribute to teachers' mechanistic focus on the low-level, rote learning methods described earlier. As critics have pointed out (Kendall & Marzano, 1995; NAEYC & NAECS/SDE, 2002; Reeves, 2002), many standards documents have emphasized isolated facts and skills, rather than engaging students in larger and more motivating "big ideas." As emphasized in the standards of the National Council of Teachers of Mathematics (NCTM, 2000), a *big idea* is a statement of an idea that is central to the learning of a particular discipline; it is an idea that links numerous understandings into a coherent, connected whole. In mathematics or in any other content area, these big ideas are more likely to promote interest, focused attention, complex problem-solving, and motivation to learn.

As described in the Introduction and in Chapter 3, some states' early learning standards do include approaches to learning as a separate standards category. Other states embed various components of approaches to learning within other standards categories such as social studies or social and emotional competence (Scott-Little, Kagan, & Frelow, 2005). However, when "approaches to learning" is not identified as a distinct standards category, such embedded references may not make educators and other decision makers sufficiently aware of this school readiness domain.

Policies Related to High-Stakes Assessment

Certainly, not all forms of assessment run the risk of undermining children's positive approaches to learning. In fact, a position statement from two national organizations (NAEYC & NAECS/SDE, 2003) asserts that assessment is every child's right and that, at its best, assessment supports positive outcomes, giving educators essential information to inform their teaching. For children with disabilities, assessment has additional value, making it possible to access services and to create and evaluate individualized education plans, or IEPs (Division for Early Childhood, 2007).

Despite these potential benefits, many policies related to assessment and accountability do indeed create risks for children; in fact, awareness of those trends is what motivated national organizations to speak out in position statements and other venues. One of the real dangers of inappropriate assessment is that it can undermine children's enthusiasm and engagement in learning.

For example, because many of the assessments now mandated by state or federal agencies emphasize a narrow range of basic skills, teachers may feel that those are the areas that they must emphasize, to the exclusion of broader competencies and more potentially engaging material. Because "teaching to the test" in effect becomes the curriculum, the curriculum moves in an ever-narrower and less challenging direction. The pattern is seen from the early years through secondary school. The National Research Council's (2003) report on engagement among high school students found that, faced with the need to prepare students for multiple-choice tests of isolated facts, teachers were focusing less on meaningful, cognitively challenging material—and, in turn, students were less engaged.

Especially as children get older, they are likely to internalize the current obsession with test results. In today's policy climate, teachers and parents start early to lecture children about the importance of high-stakes tests. With messages coming from all directions, children may see the whole purpose of education as getting ready to perform well on these tests. In this assessment climate, children are likely to develop "performance goals" rather than the mastery or learning goals that are linked with positive approaches to learning (Dweck, 2000), and their motivation to learn is likely to become extrinsic rather than intrinsic.

IMPACT ON THE MOST VULNERABLE CHILDREN

The influences described in this chapter are not good for any young children, but they are most likely to adversely affect children who are already at risk. These children need the added boost of positive approaches to learning, but instead they are the least likely to receive those benefits.

Children with Disabilities

Although children with disabilities are less likely to become engaged than are typically developing children, early intervention can promote their engagement and, therefore, their learning (McWilliam et al., 1985). However, in this chapter we have seen examples of curriculum and classroom practices that undermine engagement for all children, and that can be expected to have an especially detrimental effect for children who need very intentional engagement strategies. Recall Rodney, one of Ms. Manning's students, who has a significant cognitive delay. We saw Rodney staring into space during the Christopher Columbus lesson, in a class where a disengaging curriculum and disengaging teaching practices are the norm. During the lesson, most of the children eventually became disengaged, but engagement matters even more for Rodney. His lack of engagement has even more negative consequences for his learning.

Children with Low Achievement

Many young children enter child care, Head Start, or prekindergarten already "behind" in their basic cognitive and academic skills (Klein & Knitzer, 2006). As we have seen, intrinsic motivation to learn propels children to master difficult material and to persist in the face of difficulties. However, some researchers have found, and practitioners have confirmed, that high-stakes accountability pressures have been especially detrimental to the motivation of children who begin school already with low achievement in comparison with other children, and who are disaffected by school, even in the early grades (Kumar, Gheen, & Kaplan, 2002). The National Research Council's (2003) report on the engagement and motivation of high school students asserts that high-stakes testing is one of the root causes of disengagement and dropout among low-achieving adolescents. Rather than motivating engagement and learning, the threat of these tests and the overriding emphasis on performance undermine at-risk students' motivation and their belief in their own competence.

Children Who Are Ethnically, Culturally, and Linguistically Diverse

Ethnic, cultural, or linguistic diversity does not in itself place children's approaches to learning at risk. However, when children's ethnicity, culture, or language differs from or is not well understood by their early education program, then there may be risks to their enthusiasm and engagement in learning. Research suggests that ethnic minority boys are especially likely to develop motivational difficulties in school—not because of an intrinsic lack of motivation, but because the curriculum content or instructional practices may fail to respond to their interests and interaction styles (Barbarin, 2002; Graham & Taylor, 2002).

More generally, the risks and difficulties may stem from a lack of fit between what the child's family expects and what the school expects in terms of appropriate learning behaviors. Teachers may interpret certain behaviors as showing a lack of interest in learning, when the behaviors are actually appropriate within the child's culture and community. For example, if children do not look directly at teachers, teachers sometimes assume that the child is resistant or uninterested in learning. Or children may have been taught at home not to ask questions of adults. One observational study of parent–teacher conferences in a predominantly

Hispanic elementary school found that an Anglo teacher told many parents that she was concerned that their child was not interested in what was being taught, because the child did not ask any questions (Greenfield, Quiroz, & Raeff, 2000). Parents were puzzled about why this culturally appropriate behavior and this "learning by listening" were criticized by their child's teacher.

Children Living in Poverty

Finally, children living in poverty—whatever their ethnicity, culture, language, or disability status—are at risk of failing to develop positive approaches to learning. Some of these risks are associated with the generally lower health and nutritional status of poor children: It is very difficult to focus attention or persist at a difficult problem when you are hungry or sick. Family stress in poor communities may also create risks for insecure relationships with adults, which in turn undermine children's ability to explore, solve problems, and take on new learning challenges.

LOOKING BACK AND LOOKING FORWARD

Like the vignette that opened the chapter, the entire content of this chapter has been disheartening. It has piled up one thing after another that can contribute to young children becoming increasingly discouraged and disengaged in learning. This is certainly bad news for teachers, administrators, advocates, and everyone who cares about young children's well-being. But the good news is that these patterns are not inevitable, nor are they irreversible. In the chapters in Part II, I will describe specific tools that early childhood educators can use to promote positive approaches to learning.

 Reflection, Discussion, and Action

1. What do experienced teachers think about these issues? Interview several whom you know, exploring their own experiences with factors and trends that may be undermining children's enthusiasm and engagement in learning.

2. Spend time observing in several classrooms, focusing on children who seem especially disengaged or resistant to involvement in learning activities. Reflecting on the factors that can undermine positive approaches to learning, consider what may be influencing these children's negative approaches to learning.

PART II

Transforming Risks into Opportunities

Evidence-Based Tools to Support Positive Approaches to Learning

I ended Part I of this book with a description of the many ways in which young children's positive approaches to learning are being ignored or even undermined. But I also emphasized that a negative outcome is not inevitable. In Part II we will examine many concrete strategies and action steps that early childhood educators can use to build children's enthusiasm and engagement, to enlist their families in this process, and to advocate for educational policies that will support positive approaches to learning.

These strategies or tools are evidence-based (Buysse & Wesley, 2005); that is, they are drawn from credible research and also from the values and experience of early childhood professionals. They can also be applied in many settings and with diverse children and families. Yet the chapters to follow will not advocate a cookie-cutter approach. As the tools are presented, I will give examples of how they may be adapted to children's developmental levels, individual and cultural characteristics, and abilities and disabilities. The strategies also need to be adapted to teachers' own styles, methods, and experiences.

I have organized this presentation of tools to support positive approaches to learning into six chapters. Chapter 5 focuses on day-to-day strategies to create and strengthen positive relationships characterized by warmth and involvement combined with high expectations. Chapter 6 is designed to help readers identify, analyze, and implement curriculum that will promote positive approaches to learning. The emphasis in Chapter 7 is on the physical environment, scheduling, and grouping decisions; teachers as models; and teaching practices that build children's intrinsic motivation, engagement, and self-regulation. Chapter 8 affirms the central place of assessment in quality early childhood education, emphasizing the way in which assessment results may tell us more about children's approaches to learning and therefore inform decisions about curriculum and teaching. The focus in Chapter 9 is on how early childhood educators can create reciprocal relationships with families, engage in focused conversations about their children's approaches to learning, and share practical ideas with families in respectful, culturally responsive ways. Chapter 10 takes readers beyond the classroom and family contexts to explore other ways in which the early childhood profession can ensure greater attention to children's approaches to learning—through new research agendas, professional development, and public policies.

Within the chapters in Part II you will find materials such as the following:

- Concrete examples of the tools, so that you can see how they might be implemented in various settings
- "Research Reminders": Brief notes about the research base related to these strategies
- "Nuts and Bolts": Quick tips for putting each strategy into daily practice
- "Enhancing the Everyday": Samples of classroom situations, lesson plans, teaching interactions, and other everyday events—with invitations to analyze, improve, and adapt them.

Let's start by identifying how your relationships with children—and their membership in learning communities—can support their enthusiasm and engagement.

5 Tools to Build Closer Relationships with All Children

Serena, the co-teacher of this prekindergarten group, is sitting at a table early in the morning. Gradually, children enter and find things to do. Serena has put out a large container of Legos and has been joined by two girls: Mariel and Lucy. Serena builds right along with the children, talking to herself as she does: "Oh, maybe I can use a few of those pieces instead," and "I don't have any windows yet. Hmmm . . . I wonder where I can put them. Let's see."

A little later Tanika arrives and drifts shyly over to the table, looking over Serena's shoulder. "Oh, good morning, Tanika!" Serena says welcomingly. "Here's a seat for you. I would love to hear about your grandmother's visit. Did her bus get in on time? Do you think you and Grana are going to visit Mommy at the hospital this afternoon?" As the play time goes on, Serena engages children in conversation about their own structures. To Mariel, who had looked discouraged at her building efforts, she comments, "That is getting really tall. What are you going to do to keep it from falling down? Oh, I see now—that makes sense." Looking at what Lucy is creating, Serena gestures to the other two children, drawing them into noticing and appreciating Lucy's way of building, and eventually engaging them in making a group structure as they figure out how to connect their "houses."

When Wendell, the other teacher, lets the group know that it's time to clean up for break-fast, Serena says to the girls, "Is there something that you would like to put on the saving shelf to work on later?"

S SEEN IN THE RESEARCH referred to in Chapters 3 and 4, relationships are critically important for every aspect of young children's development (Howes & Ritchie, 2002; Shonkoff & Phillips, 2000), including their enthusiasm for and engagement in learning. Thus, this first chapter in Part II focuses on the tools for building closer relationships with all children. Figure 5.1 provides a brief reminder of the influences relationships can have on children's positive approaches to learning—influences that are seen in the opening vignette and that will be further illustrated in the rest of this chapter. First I will describe two tools: *connections*—personal warmth, sensitivity, and involvement with individual children—and *community*—a classroom and school where all children are accepted and appreciated. The chapter will then show how close relationships can have a specific impact on children who are experiencing difficulties in learning and in life, and will provide some thoughts about teachers' own relationships.

> ◆ **Goals of This Chapter**
>
> After reading this chapter, you will be better able to
>
> 1. Explain how relationships support children's enthusiasm and engagement in learning.
> 2. Implement specific strategies to create better teacher–child relationships and a better sense of classroom community.
> 3. Tap into the power of relationships—connections and community—as ways to support the positive approaches to learning of children who are experiencing special difficulties.

TOOL 1: CONNECTIONS WITH CHILDREN

Early childhood educators often enter the field because they have experienced the joy of warm relationships with young children, or because they look forward to having these relationships. Being closely connected with children seems to come naturally for many of us. But, as in other aspects of teaching, a more intentional focus on what "seems to come naturally" is an investment worth making (see Figure 5.2).

❧ FIGURE 5.1   Research Reminders: Relationships and Approaches to Learning

- When teachers establish emotionally secure relationships with children, these relationships contribute to children's engagement in school (Morrison, 2007).
- In elementary school, children's descriptions of their relationships with their teachers predict children's coping behavior, feelings of autonomy, and engagement in school (Furrer & Skinner, 2003).
- Teachers' reported closeness to individual children predicts children's academic success (Pianta, 2000).
- Children who report a greater sense of "relatedness" to their school show more emotional and behavioral engagement in learning (Furrer & Skinner, 2003).
- If teachers show more positive emotion and sensitivity, and are less harsh and detached, young children are more likely to be engaged in the classroom (Ridley et al., 2000).
- Even in high school, if children feel that the teacher cares about them, they put forth more effort for that teacher (National Research Council, 2003).

❧ FIGURE 5.2   Nuts and Bolts: Fostering Teacher–Child Connections

- Smile when you make eye contact with a child during the day.
- Touch children affectionately but in ways that are individually and culturally appropriate.
- When you're listening to a child, turn your whole body toward the child.
- When you end a conversation with a child, pause for a moment and keep looking at the child before turning to something else—you'll affirm that the child and the conversation are important to you.
- Ask a child about something you know she finds important: "How did you and your daddy like that movie you saw over the weekend?"
- Sincerely compliment a child's effort, not just the result: "You were really working hard on that puzzle—I could see how hard you tried."
- Share things from your own experiences when you're teaching about something— for example, when studying the sea: "When I was your age, we lived near the ocean, and I'd take walks on the beach."
- Let children see that you're not perfect: "Oh, no! I forgot to order more paints, so we don't have the colors we usually do. Any ideas about what we can do until the order comes in?"
- Respond immediately to children's bullying, harassment, or put-downs of others, so as to create an emotionally safe environment for all.

Adapted from Bluestein (2001), Hyson (2004), and Kirschen (2005).

Knowledge of Children and Their Families

Connections with children are strengthened when teachers have personal knowledge of the children they teach, their families, and their communities. Serena's knowledge is evident in the way that she welcomes children to the Lego table and weaves personal comments into her conversation, as she did in talking with Tanika about her grandmother's visit and her mother's hospitalization.

Especially if they do not live in the community where they teach, teachers may walk or ride around the community, noticing where the children spend their time, how they walk to school, where their families shop, what bus routes they travel on, and so on. Some teachers are able to make home visits before children begin attending their program, using this time to get a sense of families' hopes and dreams for their children, their parenting practices, and their everyday lives. However this information is gathered, it's important to keep attuned to whether families are comfortable sharing information, especially if cultural differences exist. A welcoming, sensitive, respectful attitude can build trust over time. (Chapter 9 provides many suggestions for how to connect with and involve families in promoting their children's positive approaches to learning.)

Of course, children are able to communicate a good deal about themselves and their lives outside of school, once they become able to express themselves in words or through drawing and other media. By making time to talk personally with each child, every day, teachers can expand their knowledge of individual members of their class. This can sound overwhelming to a busy teacher, but even 1 minute of focused attention can be invaluable to a child. In having these conversations, it's important not to quiz children or put them on the spot. Each child is different, and not all children are eager to share all facets of their lives at all times. Especially as children get older, they may be reluctant to share some information, and that privacy needs to be respected. Open-ended questions and comments may help: "That looks like a new jacket, Simon," or "You really gave your daddy a big, big hug when he left this morning," or "I wonder who will pick you up this afternoon, Camilla. Do you think you know?" Often children will eagerly chime in when teachers share something from their own lives: "After I go home today, we need to take my cat to the vet. He is a little sick right now."

Besides these kinds of conversations, thoughtful observation and documentation will open a window into children's unique personalities, interests, strengths, and needs. Chapter 8 describes specific ways to do this. To gather information that can help make connections with children, it is important to focus on strengths, not just areas that seem to need improvement. Whether in a notebook, on index cards, or in a computer, teachers of young children can describe and document these special qualities, which in turn provide a basis for strengthening positive bonds between teachers and children. As the children transition from their early morning free play to breakfast, Serena takes a minute to jot down notes about Lucy's increased confidence and interest in building complex structures.

Warmth and Sensitivity

Knowledge about children needs to translate into connection-building behavior. Children are quick to pick up cues about adults' feelings. They know which teachers are warm and caring. Warm teachers convey sincere liking for and appreciation of children. Depending on children's ages, cultures, and other characteristics—as well as teachers' individual styles—teachers can show warmth in many ways. Kind expressions, welcoming smiles, gentle touches, a nurturing tone of voice—all of these send messages about how adults feel about being around children in general, and individual children as well.

Related to expressions of warmth are teacher behaviors that communicate and reflect sensitivity. Teachers who are sensitive respond "contingently" to individual children and to the changing interests and needs of a group of children. Why is this so important? When an adult responds contingently to a child's comments, tone of voice, behavior, or mood, the child's sense of being known and valued is affirmed. Sensitive teachers stop, look, and listen to what children are doing, and they are able to make meaningful connections with children's behavior. Serena made a point of talking to herself—in Mariel's hearing—as she tried to deal with her own challenges in fixing her Lego structure, having seen that Mariel has been frustrated lately in implementing her very ambitious plans.

Involvement with Children

Connections with children are also enhanced when teachers get directly involved in what children are doing, especially when the activity is not teacher-planned. A teacher can sit with one child or a small group, giving them just a bit of help when they need it, and communicating by the teacher's presence that she values the child and the child's activity. For example, when Serena noticed that Mariel looked discouraged, Serena was able to create a warm climate while also modeling positive learning behaviors: "Oh, I'm not sure I'm going to be able to put a door in this house I'm building. I wonder what pieces I could try? Whoops, that one doesn't fit. What about this one, do you think?" This kind of involvement certainly scaffolds children's cognitive and academic development, but it also contributes significantly to the adult–child relationship.

During these kinds of episodes and in other ways, teachers can also let children know that they view the children as smart, competent, and able to succeed through their own efforts and with the help of others. Involved teachers give children specific feedback and acknowledgment of their efforts and behavior: "Thank you so much for throwing those paper cups away. Now the table's all ready for our painting project." Notice that these messages should be concrete, rather than the kind of vague, global praise that can actually undermine intrinsic motivation (Dweck, 2000). When children are from diverse cultures and may speak a language other than English, it's important that the teacher's affirmation is culturally responsive—for example, one child may stand silently, head bowed,

> ## ❥ FIGURE 5.3   Enhancing the Everyday: Teacher–Child Connections
>
> Here is an everyday situation that could be enhanced to increase its focus on teacher–child connections, which are so critical for building positive approaches to learning.
>
> *Two-year-old Elias and his mother have recently moved from another part of the state. He has just begun attending the Fair Winds family child care home. Elias seems very shy. He shakes his head "no" when invited to join in any of the free choice activities that Ms. Yolanda offers. So far he has spent much of his time just sitting in a corner holding a stuffed rabbit that he brings from home. Ms. Yolanda has tried holding Elias on her lap during group times or other activities, but he pushes her away and has sometimes even started to cry. Even when she smiles at him or pats him on the back he turns from her.*
>
> What are some things you would suggest to Ms. Yolanda to create a positive relationship with Elias—a relationship that will then help him become more enthusiastic and engaged in his new program?

rather that calling the teacher's attention to how well she is cleaning up. Tuned in to this style, the teacher may give a warm, sincere "Gracias!" or may acknowledge the help of the group of children, not just the individual.

Having read about Tool 1, you might read the vignette in Figure 5.3 and consider how you would answer the question in light of what you know about relationships.

TOOL 2: COMMUNITY—WHERE CHILDREN ARE ACCEPTED, ACKNOWLEDGED, AND APPRECIATED

In addition to creating connections with individual children, early childhood educators can strengthen another aspect of relationships: what has been called a "Caring Community of Learners" (Bredekamp & Copple, 1997).

What Are Caring Communities, and Why Are They Important?

Caring communities have been defined as "places where teachers and students care about and support each other, actively participate in and contribute to activities and decisions, feel a sense of belonging and identification, and have a shared sense of purpose and common values" (Lewis, Schaps, & Watson, 1995, p. 547). Although the details may vary depending on the specific setting as well as on children's ages, cultures, and other characteristics, this description gets at the heart of the concept.

Close connections with teachers are the most essential relationships, but especially as children get older, being part of a caring community provides an expanded sense of *belonging* and *importance*, both as a unique individual and as a valued member of a group. Community may extend not only to the classroom but also to the entire school and, indeed, the wider community—the neighborhood, town, or village. Belonging to such a community may be especially valuable for children whose cultures emphasize interdependence and shared rather than individual effort. For all children, research in elementary and secondary schools repeatedly shows that schools that emphasize this sense of community foster greater self-direction and stronger motivation to learn—key components of children's positive approaches to learning (Northwest Education Collaborative, 2001). The same benefits are likely to be seen in programs serving younger children.

Starting Small: Ways to Create Caring Communities

Just as with teacher–child relationships, caring communities are built from small actions. Perhaps most important is for teachers to be models for children, using the kind of respectful, inclusive language and behavior that teachers would like children to learn to use (Diffily & Sassman, 2002). As Figure 5.4 suggests, everyday interactions and small changes in everyday activities can give children

---

❧ FIGURE 5.4   Nuts and Bolts: Tips for Creating Caring Communities

Here are some suggestions for ways that early childhood educators can help create caring communities of learners. Of course, each should be considered in light of children's developmental levels, cultures, and abilities or disabilities.

◆ Model respectful language for children to use with one another: "Thank you for helping YuYu pick up her bristle blocks. That made it easier for her to finish up, and for all of us to get ready to go outside."

◆ Identify individual children's interests and talents that can help the whole group: "Elsa is our expert on how to tie shoes. If you're having trouble, try asking her!" or "Maybe Leo remembers how to play that game—I think he was playing this morning."

◆ Try to say, "That's a decision you can make together," instead of always making the decisions for children.

◆ Teach children how to listen and contribute in group discussions: looking at the person who's speaking, waiting to speak, and so forth.

◆ Create shared rituals that reflect "the way we do things in our class": a special story hour every Friday; a handshake as children leave, and so forth.

◆ Use cooking projects as ways of building and celebrating community, especially if these can involve children of different ages and cultural traditions (Howell, 1999).

◆ Find concrete ways—such as a "kindness jar," a display board, or acknowledgments during a daily group time—to help children notice and describe kind things that others do to make the class a better place for everyone.

Adapted from Diffily and Sassman (2002) and Whitin (2001).

messages about their value as community members and about the behaviors and attitudes that make a group of individuals a supportive community. Watching Serena with the three girls at the Lego table, one could sense the comfortable sense of community that was being created, simply in Serena's tone of voice, in her genuine welcome, and in the low-key way that she invited children to show each other how they were building and to try making something together.

Next Steps: Big Jobs, Projects, and Class Meetings

Beyond the daily nuts and bolts of community-building, teachers can consider other steps. The next sections describe just three of many possibilities: (1) the use of "Big Jobs," (2) project work, and (3) class meetings.

Big Jobs for small children.   Most early childhood programs use "jobs" as one of their regular classroom rituals. Children are assigned or volunteer for jobs such as feeding the fish, wiping the tables, or being line leader. Although these can be worthwhile activities, they are often done by individuals, are sometimes make-work, and have limited potential to contribute to a sense of community. A next step may be to consider Big Jobs—tasks that are both challenging and essential to the program. In a recent article (Jones, 2005), for example, teachers in a rural preschool described their use of Big Jobs that involved children in hauling feed for animals in wagons, shoveling snow off the steps of the school, and other activities that require teamwork and are clearly essential for the school's functioning. Whatever the setting, these kinds of jobs help children gain a sense of competence and efficacy, as they see how their shared hard work helps the larger community.

Project work.   Project work, which involves children in an extended study of a topic, has become part of many early childhood programs from preschool through the primary grades. Sometimes this work is an integral component of a curriculum framework such as the Project Approach (Helm & Katz, 2001; Katz & Chard, 2000) or the Reggio Emilia approach (Edwards, Gandini, & Forman, 1998). Other teachers may use projects, themes, or integrated instructional units in a more general way (Diffily & Sassman, 2002). Among the many benefits of project work is its contribution to a sense of community, which in turn promotes enthusiastic, engaged learning. Project work offers teachers the opportunity to bring children together in collaborative investigations. As the project takes shape with children's input, each child's contributions will differ depending on the child's interests and skills. These individual contributions come together, culminating in a community exhibition, documentation, or celebration of learning.

Class meetings.   Beyond routine circle times, class meetings can be designed to make key contributions to children's sense of community, which in turn sets the stage for more enthusiastic and engaged participation in learning activities.

⬙ FIGURE 5.5   Enhancing the Everyday: Show and Tell

Here is another everyday situation that could be enhanced. In this case, the goal is to more effectively use a ritual to build a caring community of learners.

In this kindergarten class, as in many others, every Monday the children have Show and Tell. In this ritual, children may bring something from home—usually a toy, but other things may be brought to school as well—to show and describe to their class-mates. The children enjoy this activity, although sometimes they have a hard time listening to one another. Sometimes, also, children become competitive, vying to bring things that are bigger and better than the toys brought the previous week by their friends.

The kindergarten teachers would like to make some changes in the way they do Show and Tell. How might the activity be modified to create a greater sense of classroom community, belonging, importance, and acceptance for all children?

Early childhood educators have many different formats and purposes for class meetings (Educators for Social Responsibility, 2007). An important purpose is to help children engage in discussions about classroom problems—whether these are conflicts between children, perceived unfairness of a classroom rule, or a child's feelings of exclusion from a group of friends. Gathering together regularly to engage in this sort of dialogue, under the guidance of adults who model caring and respect, helps build a "peaceable classroom" to which all children belong and can contribute (Levin, 2003; Vance & Weaver, 2002).

Over time, teachers usually find that classroom conflicts are reduced, and the energy that was going into those problems can be used for productive learning. Furthermore, skills in social problem-solving and self-regulation, emphasized in activities such as class meetings, carry over to other times of the day, where they contribute to children's overall positive approaches to learning. By working together on real, not contrived, problems during a class meeting, children come to appreciate one another's thinking and enjoy arriving at a group solution to the problem—a solution that contributes to the welfare of the entire group, not just to an individual's success. Whatever the format or the issues being discussed (see the example in Figure 5.5), class meetings are yet another way to build this sense of community and thereby create relationships that can support children's positive approaches to learning.

CRITICAL TIMES WHEN RELATIONSHIPS CAN MAKE THE DIFFERENCE

Relationships are always important, but at times they may have special significance in supporting children's positive approaches to learning.

When Learning Is Hard

All children find learning difficult at times. At these times, they may have a great deal of trouble staying interested, focused, and engaged. Even in the hands of sensitive teachers and with an appropriate curriculum, some skills are inherently hard to learn (e.g., tying one's shoes was before the era of Velcro). With few exceptions, children find learning to read difficult, as one can see watching a typical first-grader laboriously sounding out an unfamiliar word. Learning to write can also be frustrating, especially for children whose fine motor skills may lag behind those of their classmates.

While certain aspects of learning are hard for almost all children, other domains present more individual difficulties. A child who takes easily to reading may have a hard time with mathematical concepts. Another child may find it difficult to learn motor skills such as "pumping" on the swings. A child who has attention deficit disorder will be frustrated by her efforts to sit quietly for the longer circle time in her new classroom, and a child with learning disabilities may be discouraged when trying to spell words that are easy for classmates.

In these situations, children are at risk of becoming discouraged, losing confidence in their own competence, and failing to exert the sustained effort needed to master difficult concepts or skills. These are exactly the times when prior investments in relationships—those teacher–child connections and that caring community of learners—will pay off, giving children a boost over the rough spots and encouraging them to persist until things get easier. For all children, but especially for children with disabilities who may be struggling with learning, a positive emotional climate in the classroom has been shown to promote greater engagement and higher levels of engagement (Dilcher & Hyson, 1997).

When Life Is Hard

Connections and community can also help children maintain their enthusiasm and engagement in learning during difficult times in their lives. Some children's lives seem to be unrelentingly hard: These children may experience extreme poverty, continuing violence in their communities, and other chronic sources of stress. Other children may go through shorter periods of hardship—for example, parents may separate, a mother may be laid off from work, or a child may have a health crisis.

These kinds of risk factors can interfere with children's ability to develop positive approaches to learning. But the good news is that research also shows the power of relationships to "buffer" these kinds of chronic or intermittent stress. For example, researchers have found that African American children's language skills were enhanced when they had a more positive relationship with their teacher, as compared with children whose teacher–child relationships were poor (Burchinal, Peisner-Feinberg, Pianta, & Howes, 2002). Teachers' intentional emphasis on these relationships—often by promoting greater family involvement and by creating an especially positive emotional climate—can reverse negative trends and begin positive cycles. Serena, the teacher in our opening vignette, creates warm relationships with all children, but she is especially attuned to those like Tanika who are experiencing multiple stresses.

In both of these challenging situations—when learning is hard and when life is hard (or, for many children, when both are hard)—an early childhood program can be a "protective shield" (Northwest Education Collaborative, 2001). Not only personal relationships with teachers but also a general sense of belonging can create a safe haven for children, giving them the emotional security that makes it possible for them to focus on something other than the anxiety, distress, or chaos in their lives.

Teachers' Feelings and Relationships

A chapter on relationships cannot end without looking at teachers' own emotions and relationships, and how these may affect their connections with children. The tools that have been recommended in this chapter depend on teachers' ability to be emotionally available to children. The reality is that this can be difficult when teachers are themselves struggling with depression, anxiety, or other psychosocial stressors (Li-Grining et al., 2007). Teachers who are experiencing problems such as depression are less likely to have the kinds of close relationships with children that promote their enthusiasm and engagement in learning. The way to address these kinds of issues is not to urge teachers to cheer up, but to use the same kind of sensitive support with teachers that we recommend using with children. Supervisors and colleagues can often identify teachers who have emotional difficulties or are at risk for developing difficulties, and then provide extra support for them and, if necessary, refer them to professionals who can help. At the same time, it's important to look at the conditions within which teachers work. Sometimes what gets in the way of relationship-building is not a teacher's individual mental health but a climate of low wages, low respect, and unsupportive working conditions.

LOOKING BACK AND LOOKING FORWARD

Serena's time with the small group of children at the Lego table illustrates the power of relationships in supporting positive approaches to learning. With her warmth, responsiveness, and ability to create a learning community, Serena is not only enhancing children's pleasure at being in her class but also using these relationships to enhance their motivation to learn, persistence, interest, and other components of enthusiasm and engagement. As this chapter has emphasized, these relationships are the most basic tools needed to develop enthusiastic and engaged young learners. The next chapter will add another set of tools—those provided by effective early childhood curriculum.

Reflection, Discussion, and Action

1. You might spend time observing in several early childhood programs. As you compare these, what evidence do you see of an emphasis on relationships—that is, on connections and community? What specific activities or interactions give you this evidence?

2. In these same programs, do you see linkages between what's happening in teachers' relationships with individual children—or in the caring community of learners—and children's degree of enthusiasm and engagement in learning?

3. Think about a child for whom learning is hard or for whom life is hard. How are relationships helping this child become more enthusiastic and engaged in learning? If this is not happening, how might relationships support more positive approaches to learning?

4. Imagine that you are meeting with policy makers at the local, district, or state level. You're advocating for more training and support for teachers around relationship-building. The policy makers are skeptical about how this would help children meet standards. What would be your key points in a concise presentation?

5. Throughout this chapter we have emphasized that strategies for building relationships need to be adapted to children's ages, individual abilities and needs, the specific program setting, and other characteristics. Select one of the chapter's suggestions and consider its relevance to children with whom you may work. How appropriate might this suggestion be, and are there adaptations that would make it more effective?

6 ◆ Tools to Find and Use More Effective Curriculum

In an earlier chapter we met the 4-year-olds in Serena's prekindergarten class as they began their morning. Now the children are finishing breakfast and preparing for their first group meeting of the day. The curriculum in this school does not follow only one model. Over the years, the director and the teaching staff have adapted elements of one comprehensive curriculum and added elements of others, as they also draw upon their long experience in the community.

Serena uses the group meeting to describe the areas that are available for children to choose during the next block of time. Some of these areas reflect standard features of the curriculum, but new elements are regularly added based on the teachers' goals and children's interests. "When we choose our areas, there will be one where you can make fishing rods to use in the rocking boat."

Because Zachary has brought a book from home, Serena agrees to read it to the class. It is a small book, so she tells the children that she will bring the book around the circle so that they can all see it. She reminds them to "Get your listening and thinking cap on [throwing imaginary caps to some children]: Rub it, stretch it, put it on, rub your ears so they can hear, and rub your eyes so they will see well."

After the story the children choose centers in which to work and play. After the group time ends and children begin to circulate around the room, a few have already forgotten which area they chose. Serena is able to check her list and guide them to do what they had planned. In the block area several boys have taken out tape measures (measurement is an emphasis in the math part of the curriculum at this time of the year). Serena asks them what they want to measure and helps them carry out their ideas.

N THIS CHAPTER I will suggest ways to identify, analyze, and implement curriculum that will promote positive approaches to learning. We will look both at curriculum that is "comprehensive" (curriculum models that address all areas of development) and at curriculum that is more content- or discipline-specific (science curriculum being an example).

The discussion will begin with information from research about how valuable early childhood curricula can be in supporting children's engagement, interest, persistence, and other learning behaviors. However, not all curricula provide such support, and any curriculum can be further enhanced. To help early childhood programs use their curricula to the greatest advantage, I will describe three tools and illustrate them with examples.

The first is a tool to analyze various early childhood curriculum models for their emphasis on approaches to learning. The second tool includes ways to adapt a currently used curriculum to give greater emphasis to positive approaches to learning. The last tool offers a way of thinking about curricula or interventions that may specifically target children's approaches to learning.

Goals of This Chapter

After reading this chapter, you will be better able to

1. Review published curricula in terms of their potential to promote positive approaches to learning.

2. Make specific adaptations to existing curricula (either an entire curriculum or specific features within a curriculum) to focus on one or more components of children's positive approaches to learning.

3. Make additional adaptations to ensure approaches-to-learning curriculum effectiveness for children who differ in their abilities, disabilities, culture, or language characteristics.

4. Apply specific criteria when considering how to use a targeted approaches-to-learning curriculum or intervention.

WHY DO WE CARE ABOUT CURRICULUM?

A chapter on curriculum should start by describing what "curriculum" is. A simple definition is that curriculum includes *what children should know and how they should be taught.* In the early childhood field, and in this book, "curriculum" is the most general term, while "*the* curriculum" or "*a* curriculum" usually refers to one specific curriculum developed or adopted by a program. In its early childhood program standards, NAEYC (2005a) describes curriculum as including *goals* for the knowledge and skills to be acquired by children and the *plans* for learning experiences through which such knowledge and skills will be achieved—all of which are part of the curriculum implemented in Serena's program.

This definition suggests that the goals and plans of a curriculum may include emphasis on promoting children's positive approaches to learning. As noted in Chapter 3, early childhood curricula can be a key force in helping all children develop these behaviors and dispositions. On the other hand, as we saw in Chapter 4, an ineffective or inappropriate curriculum may actually undermine children's enthusiasm and engagement.

Figure 6.1 calls attention to some evidence about the features of curricula that are likely to support various components of positive approaches to learning. Researchers tend to find that a curriculum that supports children's engagement, motivation to learn, and interest

- Is challenging
- Has content that is worth learning
- Emphasizes content that connects with children's interests and experiences
- Emphasizes active participation and social interaction

Even the brief description of Serena's class suggests that the curriculum has these features. However, it is important to note that much of the curriculum research has been done with older children and may not be directly relevant in early childhood settings.

An important point, emphasized by Wigfield and Tonks (2004) and others, is that a curriculum that is effective in developing motivation to learn and other positive approaches to learning must do more than be "motivating" or "interesting." Children must also learn important content and skills through the curriculum—not just because content and skills are valuable outcomes in themselves but because children feel more competent and have a stronger sense of self-efficacy if there are things they know and are able to do. Examples of such important, competence-building curriculum emphases are strategies to help children comprehend what they read (Wigfield & Tonks, 2004), or the measuring skills that Serena's children are learning in the block area.

With this general background, let's now look at three tools that can help early childhood professionals find and use a potentially effective curriculum.

❧ FIGURE 6.1   Research Reminders: Curriculum and Approaches to Learning

- The National Research Council's *Eager to Learn* report (Bowman, Donovan, & Burns, 2001) and others emphasize that better child outcomes occur when programs use some kind of well-defined and intentionally implemented curriculum (Hyson et al., 2006; Klein & Knitzer, 2006).
- Some claim that child-centered or constructivist models are always superior to didactic, adult-directed approaches. However, the *Eager to Learn* report did not find the overall evidence compelling, and most experts see the need for both child-initiated and teacher-initiated experiences, whatever the curriculum model (Epstein, 2006).
- In terms of motivational outcomes, however, there is some evidence that more didactic curricula may be associated with more negative outcomes on various measures of children's motivation to learn (Hirsh-Pasek, Hyson, & Rescorla, 1990; Stipek, Feiler, Daniels, & Milburn, 1995).
- Children's engagement is promoted when curriculum focuses on what is worth learning—the "big ideas" in a discipline (Brophy, 2004; National Council of Teachers of Mathematics, 2006)
- Curriculum that is integrated across subject domains seems to have a positive effect on children's overall motivation to learn (Wigfield & Tonks, 2004).

TOOL 1: ANALYSIS OF CURRICULUM MODELS

Early childhood curriculum models or approaches may differ on many dimensions, including the curriculum's explicitness or structure, its comprehensiveness, and its mix of teacher- and child-guided activities. These differences do not necessarily make one curriculum better than another. However, in a joint position statement, two national early childhood organizations urge programs to "Implement curriculum that is thoughtfully planned, challenging, engaging, developmentally appropriate, culturally and linguistically responsive, comprehensive, and likely to promote positive outcomes for all young children" (NAEYC & NAECS/SDE, 2003). In the position statement, the organizations outline specific indicators of a curriculum that is likely to promote good outcomes for children:

- Children are active and engaged
- Goals are clear and shared by all
- Curriculum is evidence-based
- Valued content is learned through investigation and focused, intentional teaching
- Curriculum builds on prior learning and experiences
- Curriculum is comprehensive
- Professional standards validate the curriculum's subject-matter content
- The curriculum is likely to benefit children

These criteria describe an effective curriculum in terms such as *challenging, engaging, valued content,* and *responsive*—terms that are similar to those we have used to describe the components of positive approaches to learning. This suggests that if an early childhood curriculum fully meets the NAEYC and NAECS/SDE criteria, the curriculum is likely (though not guaranteed) to support the development of positive approaches to learning.

With these criteria as a general guide, let us examine selected curriculum models to see the extent to which they are likely to promote positive approaches to learning. The examples were chosen for several reasons: They are relatively well known and available to programs, and in different ways each includes a relatively explicit emphasis on various components of children's approaches to learning. This discussion is not intended to endorse any of the models, or to slight others. Rather, the object is to illustrate some ways in which familiar curricula have incorporated a focus on enthusiasm and engagement. The descriptions are necessarily brief and are focused only on those aspects that are relevant to this book. The references cited in each section provide more extensive information on the specific curricula from their developers or implementers. For other perspectives on various early childhood curriculum models, see Goffin and Wilson (2001), Kessler and Swadener (1992), and Seefeldt (1999).

The examples begin with five curricula that would be considered comprehensive (i.e., curricula that were designed to address many areas of children's development and learning) and conclude with one content-specific example—a science curriculum.

Montessori Curriculum

Contemporary Montessori education has grown out of Maria Montessori's pioneering work in the early 20th century (Torrence & Chattin-McNichols, 2000). Mixed-age groups of children work independently and in small groups, often with manipulative, self-correcting materials specially designed to help children construct an understanding of concepts. Teachers observe children's development and respond by providing materials, a consistent structure, and encouragement of learning. They demonstrate the purpose and use of materials but then allow children to investigate independently.

Montessori education is premised on the belief that children are intrinsically motivated to learn and to feel deep joy in learning. One of the central tenets of Montessori education is the importance of children developing what Maria Montessori called "self-direction," or what might be termed "self-regulation" from an approaches-to-learning perspective (Montessori, 1995; Torrence & Chattin-McNichols, 2000). According to Montessori, inner discipline develops from opportunities to discover something of deep interest and to act on that interest in purposeful ways. These opportunities are intentionally built into the materials and daily routine of a Montessori classroom.

Engagement, or what Montessori called "concentration," is another key goal in the Montessori curriculum. The story is told that Maria Montessori once demonstrated to dubious visitors the power of children's concentration by watching a child who was utterly absorbed in manipulating a set of cylinders that she held in her lap. Montessori then quietly lifted up the child, chair and all, and moved her to another part of the room without the child's ever shifting attention from her self-chosen task (Montessori, 1964). This utter absorption in learning may be unusual, but an emphasis on intrinsic motivation, love of learning, persistence, and focused attention is at the heart of Montessori education.

High/Scope Curriculum

Initially influenced by Piaget's theory of development, and more generally by constructivism, the High/Scope curriculum was designed to develop children's understanding of essential concepts of space, time, number, and classification, as well as other important developmental outcomes (Hohman & Weikart, 1995). According to the developers, the curriculum is built around teacher- and child-initiated learning activities in five main curriculum content areas: approaches to learning; language, literacy, and communication; social and emotional development; physical development, health, and well-being; and arts and sciences. An important feature of this curriculum is its focus on underlying concepts or big ideas, rather than on mechanical skills. The curriculum is organized around key developmental indicators (formerly known as "key experiences"); active learning promotes understanding of these and other concepts.

Several features appear to intentionally support some of the components of approaches to learning. For example, the High/Scope curriculum has a strong emphasis on children's planning. The daily schedule is built around a so-called "plan/do/review" sequence. First, in a group meeting children are guided in planning how they will use their free-choice time in various learning areas (*plan*). Children then have substantial blocks of time to involve themselves in these activities (*do*). Following this work time, the children gather again in small or large groups to recall, represent, and reflect on their activities, using language or other media (*review*). The curriculum's emphasis on child-initiated activities is intended to support sustained interest and engagement, which are other aspects of positive approaches to learning. At the same time, teacher-initiated activities and interactions not only support conceptual and skill development but also enhance children's attention and persistence in their activities.

Tools of the Mind

The newest of the comprehensive curricula discussed in this section, Tools of the Mind (Bodrova & Leong, 2007), was developed to put into practice the developmental and educational ideas of the Russian psychologist Lev Vygotsky

(1978). Again, many of the emphases in this curriculum are consistent with and foster children's positive approaches to learning. In the preschool years, the primary goal of the curriculum is *self-regulation*, which is also seen as a key developmental accomplishment of the age group. "At the end of kindergarten, young children should be able to regulate their physical and emotional behaviors, and some of their cognitive behaviors" (Bodrova & Leong, 2007, p. 127). A variety of activities and "mediators" are designed to support children's increasing self-regulation. Because of its central role in helping children develop cognitive and social competence, make-believe play is the central activity in the Tools of the Mind preschool curriculum. Before each extended pretend play period, children engage in a "play planning" process, using drawings and scaffolded writing to represent their ideas about what and with whom they will play, which again contributes to self-regulation. During the play period itself, teachers promote children's in-depth involvement, helping them persist in and elaborate on their make-believe play ideas.

The development of self-regulation, which includes physical, emotional, and behavioral regulation, sets the stage for the later development of motivation to learn, which this theory describes as happening in the primary grades. The primary-grades curriculum emphasizes clear, explicit standards for children's performance, accompanied by helpful "mediators" and teachers' scaffolding. Intellectual curiosity or "enquiry motivation" is another important outcome during the primary grades. Although not identical to the notion of intrinsic motivation, this concept is similar and equally important (Bodrova & Leong, 2007). The environment, learning tasks, and teacher behaviors that are emphasized in the Tools of the Mind curriculum are intended to foster this intellectual curiosity.

The Creative Curriculum

Developed by Teaching Strategies (Dodge, Colker, & Heroman, 2002), the Creative Curriculum aims to support a comprehensive set of child outcomes. Several components under our approaches-to-learning umbrella—persistence, curiosity, and flexibility, for example—are included in the outcomes that this curriculum emphasizes and assesses. The results of these assessments are used in ongoing curriculum planning based on children's strengths and challenges.

The curriculum emphasizes child choice within a classroom organized around interest centers such as blocks, art, dramatic play, and literacy. The use of the term "interest centers" suggests a focus on building on children's motivation to explore and learn. Another key emphasis in the curriculum is creating a classroom community (Dodge & Bickart, 2002), which as we have seen in Chapter 5, is a potential support for children's enthusiasm and engagement in learning. A major goal of the Creative Curriculum is teaching children how to learn, through teachers' involvement with children individually and in small groups.

The Project Approach

> *"Projecks can be edukashional. Projecks can be fun."* —Travis
> (Diffily & Sassman, 2002, p. 1)

A project is an in-depth study of a particular topic. Used at all levels of education, project-based learning or "applied learning" (Diffily & Sassman, 2002) has been advocated by Katz and colleagues as a valuable approach in early childhood education programs from the preschool years through the primary grades (Chard, 1998; Helm & Katz, 2001; Katz & Chard, 2000).

In project-based learning, children work together as they investigate problems or questions that are meaningful to their lives. They define the questions they wish to explore, track down information in developmentally appropriate ways, and share their learning with others through presentations or other kinds of documentation. Those who have developed and implemented this approach to curriculum describe children gaining a deeper knowledge of content, as well as better research and problem-solving abilities.

Additionally, the Project Approach is seen by its developers as having a number of benefits that map onto the components of approaches to learning. For example, project work is said to increase children's self-direction and motivation to learn. Positive learning dispositions (Katz, 1993, 1995) may be strengthened when children engage in extended, meaningful project work. Interest and joy in learning are likely to be stimulated because of the topics chosen by the class to investigate. And because projects take place over time, children are called on to focus their attention and to persist in sometimes challenging learning tasks.

Young Scientist Series

Each of the preceding five curricula addresses multiple areas of children's development and learning. Increasingly, however, programs, school districts, or states are turning to subject- or content-specific curricula in areas such as literacy, mathematics, and science. Sometimes these curricula supplement a comprehensive curriculum, and sometimes a set of content-specific curricula is used in place of a comprehensive curriculum.

One example of a content-specific curriculum that incorporates many of the approaches-to-learning emphases is the Young Scientist curriculum (Chalufour & Worth, 2003, 2004, 2005). With support from the National Science Foundation, the series, designed for children ages 3–5, includes curriculum guides in three areas: discovering nature, building structures, and exploring water. Whatever the topic, the teaching plans outlined in this curriculum always have three phases, starting with "Engage"—an initial whole-group time for the teacher to spark children's interest in the materials that will be available. Then considerable time, up to an hour a day, is provided for children to "Explore" the materials. Teachers use this time to support children's problem-solving efforts, sustained attention, and persistence in challenging tasks (such as using a turkey baster to pull water in and squirt it out). The interests children develop during these open explorations may then lead to focused explorations of phenomena such as water drops. In the last phase, teachers can "Extend" the explorations into other, related areas of the curriculum. In approaches-to-learning terms, the curriculum strengthens dispositions as well as helping children construct understandings of scientific phenomena. "Scientific dispositions" that are emphasized in this curriculum, and that are part of the National Science Teachers Association's standards, include curiosity, eagerness to explore, an open mind (which in approaches-to-learning terms might be considered flexibility), and delight in being a builder, an explorer, or a discoverer.

Taking a Closer Look

Whether you are already using one of these curricula or are considering adopting one of them, you will need to go beyond these brief descriptions to analyze both the overall value of the curriculum and its specific attention to children's enthusiasm and engagement. The references and Web sites referred to in this chapter will give you much more information about the six curricula. Do keep in mind, however, that these are not the only curricula that might be considered for their approaches-to-learning focus. Whatever the curriculum you are thinking about, the checklist offered in Figure 6.2 may help your analysis and decision-making.

TOOL 2: ADAPTATIONS TO CURRICULUM

Ideally, early childhood educators can influence what curricula are used in their programs. As mentioned earlier, at the long-established preschool where Serena teaches, the director and staff have not only selected but also modified their curriculum over the years. Often, however, curricula are mandated at a higher level, with teachers and program directors having very little say in the process (Chapter 10 suggests ways to have greater influence). Because of such mandates, teachers may end up using curricula that do not emphasize children's enthusiasm and engagement. Although it is best to begin with a curriculum that already has a strong emphasis on approaches to learning, almost any curriculum can be modified to more effectively promote enthusiasm and engagement.

Figure 6.3 offers suggestions about how one might adapt aspects of an existing, mandated curriculum to increase the emphasis on some components of children's approaches to learning.

Age-Appropriate Adaptations

An example may illustrate both the challenges and the opportunities in adapting a curriculum for use with an age group other than the one for which it was originally designed. In their bilingual prekindergarten program, teachers Kamil

---

**❧ FIGURE 6.2   Nuts and Bolts: Reviewing Curriculum for
                    Emphasis on Approaches to Learning**

- *Overall quality.* First, review the overall description of the curriculum in light of the criteria proposed in the position statement of NAEYC and NAECS/SDE (2003), and those suggested in Frede and Ackerman's guide (2007). In general, how well does the curriculum align with these criteria?
- *Goals.* Next, review the curriculum's stated goals or outcomes for children. Do these include goals related to promoting children's enthusiasm and engagement in learning?
- *Specific approaches-to-learning language.* Read through the more specific description and desired outcomes of the experiences and activities that are part of the curriculum. To what extent do you see approaches-to-learning terminology? Do the curriculum developers talk about how the activities promote children's "interest," "engagement," "planning," "self-regulation," "motivation," or their equivalents?
- *Activities to promote enthusiasm and engagement.* Look more closely at a sampling of the activities or experiences that are part of the curriculum. Even if you don't find that specific approaches-to-learning terminology being used, do these activities or experiences seem likely to produce positive outcomes for children's enthusiasm and engagement? Or, in contrast, does the curriculum seem likely to undermine these characteristics? (You may want to refer again to Chapters 3 and 4.)
- *Summary rating.* Consider using a rating scale like the one below to summarize your reaction to the curriculum as a potential support for children's approaches to learning.

     The curriculum is:

     ❑ Very likely to support children's enthusiasm and engagement
     ❑ Somewhat likely to support enthusiasm and engagement with some additions or adaptations
     ❑ Somewhat unlikely to support enthusiasm and engagement; major additions or adaptations would be needed
     ❑ Very unlikely to support enthusiasm and engagement

---

and Elena have been asked to implement a math curriculum that was intended to be used with kindergarten and first-grade children, not with 4-year-olds (the dearth of bilingual materials led to the adoption of this curriculum, one of the few available to use in classrooms where many children speak Spanish). The curriculum is supposed to be implemented through a mix of large- and small-group instruction, with the large groups giving teachers time to introduce key concepts and demonstrate the use of materials. Kamil and Elena have found that during the large-group lessons their 4-year-olds quickly become disengaged, inattentive, and uninterested in the curriculum content. In an effort to build more positive approaches to learning, as well as enhance children's ability to learn the

---

⩔ FIGURE 6.3   Nuts and Bolts: Adapting Curriculum to Better Promote Enthusiasm and Engagement

Following are examples of ways in which some of the components of enthusiasm and engagement might be strengthened within any early childhood curriculum, even if that curriculum lacks a sufficient approaches-to-learning focus.

- *Interest.* Sometimes a curriculum teaches skills only through generalized or decontextualized examples, such as teaching letter sounds with pictures that have little meaning for the children in a particular class. To increase interest, the same content can be taught with more meaningful examples, using concrete objects (paired with printed words) that are familiar to individual children or to the group as a whole.
- *Motivation to learn.* Some curriculum guides emphasize rewarding children for completing required activities by giving stickers or prizes. Research shows that these kinds of "motivators" can actually undermine motivation to learn. You might consider eliminating the rewards; instead, the activities can be presented in a way that will give children more choices and will emphasize the goal of mastering the challenges in the activities. With these messages (and assuming the activities are inherently engaging), it's likely that children will participate without the need for external rewards.
- *Persistence.* Some curricula are organized around a series of short, isolated activities that do not encourage children to be persistent and focused in their efforts. Teachers may consider extending some activities over a period of time, perhaps linking a series of activities into a mini-project. For example, a group of counting activities from the math curriculum could all be linked into a week-long effort by the class to get ready for Family Night, as the children count chairs, cups, and napkins, and as they make a chart listing the mothers, fathers, grandparents, and others who will attend.
- *Self-regulation.* Some curricula put the teacher entirely in charge; at the other extreme, some are so open-ended that children do not have opportunities to learn to regulate or control their own movements, feelings, or thinking processes. If a music curriculum encourages children only to move however they want when the music plays, sometimes the activities might be varied so that children respond to specific directions (from the teacher or from another child), imitate the movements of another child, or freeze when the tape is paused.

---

concepts, the teachers have streamlined and sometimes eliminated the large-group math instruction, moving immediately to small groups and embedding content within these teacher-facilitated activities. The payoff has been children's greater enthusiasm for and persistence in working with the materials and tackling the challenging content.

Figure 6.4 invites you to try your hand at making modifications to a curriculum activity in another area—a simple art project—to try to promote greater enthusiasm and engagement.

> ⧩ **FIGURE 6.4**   **Enhancing the Everyday: Adapting Curriculum to Promote Positive Approaches to Learning**

To further develop your ability to get the most out of any curriculum, first read this short plan for an art activity for a group of 4-year-olds and then address the questions that follow.

* *Making paper collages*

  Materials

  - Sheets of construction paper, different colors
  - Cut-out geometric shapes, also from colored construction paper
  - Scissors
  - Glue

  The teacher will

  - Put materials out in containers on the table
  - Keep area neat, wiping up spills
  - Remind children about safe use of scissors
  - Hang completed collages to dry

  The children will

  - Choose shapes
  - Glue shapes onto paper in a pattern of their choosing

* *Enhancing this activity*

  What additions or changes might you make to this art activity, to do more to promote positive approaches to learning? What are the strengths of this activity as part of an early childhood curriculum, and where could it be improved? Specifically, could this activity be modified to focus on some components of enthusiasm and engagement? How might you adapt this activity to:

  - Create opportunities for children to develop stronger motivation to learn?
  - Encourage children's persistence?
  - Build children's ability to use flexible problem-solving skills?
  - Increase and extend children's interests?
  - Strengthen positive approaches to learning for those children who are culturally, linguistically, or ability diverse?

  (You might want to look back at Chapter 3 to see what factors are likely to support various components of approaches to learning.)

Adaptations That Respond to Diversity

The principles and criteria recommended so far will help ensure that a curriculum is generally appropriate for culturally and linguistically diverse children, as well as for children who may have disabilities or developmental delays. However, programs may need to make further adaptations to a curriculum, or to some activities within a curriculum, to ensure that all children will develop positive approaches to learning as a result.

Again, a few examples will help make the point. Kindergarten teacher Edward is using a science curriculum that seems likely to stimulate interest and engagement on the part of most children in the class. The "Water" unit includes extensive blocks of time for small groups of children to engage in exploration together, as they gather around tubs of water. However, Edward is concerned that Harry, who has autism, will not be able to sustain his engagement in the presence of other children. So Edward provides a separate container of water for Harry, with his own set of materials, close enough to the other children that they can see each other and can be encouraged to communicate about what they are doing.

Cultural adaptations may also promote greater engagement in a curriculum. For example, the curriculum that Lin's preschool has adopted includes time for each child to independently plan what he or she will do during the morning free-choice period, with the expectation that Sarah will choose blocks, Khalid puzzles, and so on. Children whose cultures have greater emphasis on collective planning and decision-making may be more responsive if the curriculum is modified to allow them to make a group plan rather than individual plans.

TOOL 3: CURRICULUM TARGETED TO APPROACHES TO LEARNING

So far, we have considered how to select or adapt existing curricula to ensure adequate emphasis on developing children's enthusiasm and engagement. But is there another approach? What about using a separate curriculum that was developed specifically to increase children's positive approaches to learning? Would such a curriculum be of value?

As states and others recognize that approaches to learning are key aspects of school readiness and that these are desired features in early childhood curriculum, it is likely that we will see targeted curricula promoting approaches-to-learning components such as interest, joy, motivation to learn, attention, persistence, flexibility, and self-regulation. Some targeted curricula might be aimed at one or two of these components, and others may have a broader scope. Whatever the specifics, it will be critical for those considering future adoption to keep in mind both potential benefits and cautions.

A potential advantage of using a curriculum that focuses specifically on approaches to learning is that it could direct greater attention to this dimension of early learning. Additionally, the likelihood of positive results is increased if the curriculum has been validated with children similar to those in the program that may be considering adoption. Curricula that are accompanied by various staff supports, such as implementation resources and professional development, are often welcomed by staff. However, such a curriculum cannot be effectively implemented in isolation from other things that are going on in the classroom. In other words, if one uses an approaches-to-learning curriculum twice a week at circle time, and if the rest of the program actually contradicts or undermines the behaviors that the specialized curriculum is emphasizing, children will be unlikely to benefit. Also, teachers often view an add-on curriculum as a burden rather than a support, so work is always needed to ensure staff buy-in and "ownership" of the innovation.

Right now, specialized approaches-to-learning curricula are not available, although one very promising model will soon be ready for adoption. The "Evidence-Based Program for Integrated Curricula" (EPIC) is being developed and evaluated for use in Head Start and other preschool programs (Fantuzzo, Gadsden, & McDermott, 2008), with support from the federal Interagency School Readiness Initiative. The EPIC curriculum integrates intentional teaching of approaches-to-learning skills with instruction in literacy and mathematics. In creating this curriculum, a team of early childhood educators and researchers developed four complete curriculum modules, each designed to teach an important learning behavior: attention control, frustration tolerance, group learning, and task approach. Each curriculum module is structured to provide multiple learning opportunities for children to practice and reinforce positive learning behaviors, and to apply them to foster the learning of literacy and mathematics skills. In this way, these fundamental skills serve as "learning links." The curriculum also emphasizes collaboration with families to promote positive learning behaviors at home as well as in school.

LOOKING BACK AND LOOKING FORWARD

This chapter has emphasized why a high-quality curriculum is essential. Research has not identified one curriculum model as superior to all others, but we have seen consensus around some key features. As educational supervisors, directors, and state agencies consider what kinds of curricula to adopt, and as teachers engage in daily curriculum implementation, approaches-to-learning considerations should be at the forefront, as they seem to be in Serena's class. In this chapter I have suggested tools to use in conducting a serious analysis of any curriculum's potential to support enthusiasm and engagement. Chapter 7 will turn to the related arena of teaching practices and interactions with children, which can be powerful ways to create greater enthusiasm and engagement.

Reflection, Discussion, and Action

1. By yourself or with colleagues, engage in an approaches-to-learning analysis of a curriculum that is being used or considered for use in a program with which you are associated. Using the criteria suggested in this chapter, what do you see as the curriculum's strengths with respect to this area of development and school readiness?

2. Similarly, you might look closely at a curriculum that is now being used in the program (this may be an overall/comprehensive curriculum or a curriculum in one content area). How could some of the goals or plans for activities in this curriculum be modified to create more opportunities for strengthening children's enthusiasm and engagement?

3. Having done this analysis, try out some of these modifications if possible. Perhaps looking ahead to Chapter 8, use some observation and documentation to see if children's enthusiasm and engagement seem to increase when you put these changes into place. If not, what else may be needed?

4. Focusing on one or two children—individuals who may be culturally and linguistically diverse, or who may have disabilities—plan and implement additional adaptations of the program's curriculum so that these children's approaches to learning will be strengthened. Again, your assessment of the results is key.

5. Consider how you might present information to a decision-making body to persuade them that they should look closely at how the curriculum they are considering addresses children's approaches to learning. Assuming that this body is not composed of early education/child development experts, how would you make your case?

7 Tools to Teach in Ways That Promote Positive Approaches to Learning

It is reading and writing time in this kindergarten class, in which the Tools of the Mind curriculum is used (Bodrova & Leong, 2007; see Chapter 6). Most of the children are at tables in groups of three or four, working on their booklets about caterpillars (caterpillars and butterflies are a current class project). Other children are sitting on the floor in pairs, reading and listening to tapes of the book The Very Hungry Caterpillar *(Carle, 1969). After they listen to the story, they are going to draw in their journals.*

The kindergarten teacher, Elise, walks around the room, stopping to talk with children from time to time. Lennie shows her his picture of a butterfly; Elise looks at it appreciatively and responds, "That's such a colorful butterfly, Lennie. But let's think about something: When you listened to the tape, what did it say to draw after you heard the story? Was it supposed to be something that the caterpillar ate? Did he eat this butterfly? I wonder what else you could draw besides the butterfly?" Lennie and Elise laugh, Lennie thinks about it, and he gets back to work.

At the tables, children are talking to each other as they write and draw in their caterpillar booklets. "How are you doing?" asks Elise as she stops at one table. "I'm done with my

sentence," Josie reports. "Hmm," says Elise. "What's missing at the top of your page, though?"
"Whoops! My name!" says Josie, adding it to the page.

Following the reading and writing time, the children clean up to the tune of their usual song and move into morning snack time, with lively conversation. As the children gather for their class meeting, a few children are still finishing their snack, but they hurry up when Elise reminds them, "Let's go, friends, you're missing the whole song" (a caterpillar song with hand motions and some sign language, which the children all enjoy).

After the song, Elise leads the children in a discussion of what they have learned about caterpillars so far. Although the class is large, the children are quiet and attentive as they listen to their classmates' ideas and watch Elise writing them on chart paper. Several times, Elise reacts to the children's ideas by saying, "Now that is a really interesting thing about caterpillars. I'd like to know more; maybe tomorrow I can find a new book to bring in to share with you."

IN CHAPTER 6, I described criteria for analyzing, selecting, or adapting curricula that are likely to enhance positive approaches to learning. But whatever curriculum is being used, certain environments and teaching practices, such as we saw in the opening vignette, will help children become more, rather than less, enthusiastic and engaged in learning (see Figure 7.1 for evidence from research).

This chapter will describe two important tools: *effective environments*—including the physical environment, scheduling, and grouping; and *effective teaching practices*—including teachers' efforts to model positive approaches to learning, to focus on the goals of learning and mastery, to provide instructional scaffolding and elaboration, and to offer children meaningful, challenging choices.

After describing these basic tools, I will discuss situations in which even more intentional strategies may be needed—including situations in which challenging behaviors get in the way of enthusiasm and engagement, and situations in which young children have already become discouraged or disengaged.

 Goals of This Chapter

After reading this chapter, you will be better able to

1. Justify and implement specific early childhood environments and teaching practices on the basis of evidence about how to support young children's positive approaches to learning.

2. Use knowledge about preventing and addressing challenging behaviors to set the stage for positive approaches to learning.

3. Modify and adapt teaching practices to support greater enthusiasm and engagement in children who are already beginning to be discouraged and disengaged.

> ❧ **FIGURE 7.1   Research Reminders: How Environments and Teaching Strategies Create Enthusiasm and Engagement**
>
> ◆ Teachers who emphasize "learning goals," or who themselves are oriented more toward mastery/learning goals than toward performance, are more likely to have children in their class who approach learning with these kinds of goals (Midgley, 2002; Wigfield & Eccles, 2002).
>
> ◆ Teachers who spend time early in the year establishing clear procedures and routines have children who become more involved in academic tasks later on (Bohn, Roehrig, & Pressley, 2004).
>
> ◆ Young children tend to be more engaged when they are organized into small groups (Rimm-Kaufman et al., 2005), although if classroom quality is high overall, children can be engaged even during large-group activities.
>
> ◆ A body of research on K–12 children's learning (summarized by Brophy, 2004) shows that when groups are small, children usually have better classroom behavior and higher achievement.
>
> ◆ De Kruif and colleagues (2000) found that teachers who were especially controlling had a lower percentage of children in their class who were actively engaged in learning activities. These "controlling" teachers spent much of their time trying to stop children's undesirable behavior, but they rarely introduced misbehaving children to new activities and they seldom acknowledged children's efforts.
>
> ◆ Studies of high school students (National Research Council, 2003) found that the same students who are very disengaged in one class may be deeply engaged when in class with another teacher. These studies and others show that engagement is not just a trait "in" the child but is promoted or undermined by characteristics of the class and the teacher.

TOOL 1: EFFECTIVE ENVIRONMENTS

Many aspects of early childhood environments are likely to support enthusiasm and engagement. Following are examples in three areas: how the physical environment is organized; how teachers establish classroom routines and scheduling; and how children are grouped.

Setting Up the Physical Environment

It has been said that the physical environment in an early childhood setting sends messages to children: about what's important, what they are to do, and how they might do it (Kritchevsky, Prescott, & Walling, 1977). Although the physical environments that are typical of different curriculum models may look quite different on the surface, the environments of all high-quality early childhood programs have many common features. These environments

- Convey a welcoming feeling
- Give clear cues about what can be done in each area of the classroom
- Provide varied spaces that let children concentrate, as well as letting them experience lively group interactions and vigorous physical activity (Curtis & Carter, 2003; Greenman, 1987, 2005; Kritchevsky et al., 1977).

A visitor to Elise's kindergarten, described in the opening vignette, sees all of these features. Especially notable are the physical cues for children: Their names are in plastic sleeves on the back of their chairs (so they can be removed as needed), "seat sacks" on the back of their chairs hold the supplies they need, and written and pictorial labels are used to show what various areas of the room are to be used for. Further, the gathering spaces are well planned and inviting: The reading area has comfortable floor-level seating, and the rug area for whole-group meetings is large enough for the movement activities that the children love.

It is easy to see how such environments contribute to developing many of the components of children's positive approaches to learning. For example, the physical environment can encourage children to express and explore their interests and can document those interests through changing displays. Reggio Emilia programs are noted for their aesthetically beautiful environments full of visual evidence of children's pursuit of their interests (Gandini, Hill, Cadwell, & Schwall, 2005). A project stimulated by butterflies in the school's garden may, over time, result in glowing paintings, models, and other artwork beautifully displayed so that both children and families can admire, reflect, and reminisce.

Similarly, the physical environment can support—or, unfortunately, undermine—children's attention and persistence. This can be an issue for any young child, but especially for children whose disabilities or developmental delays may make it hard for them to focus. One of the children in Elise's kindergarten is on the autism spectrum. Although Arief becomes overwhelmed by social interactions, he loves to demonstrate his reading ability. After creating a quiet corner for her "sentence builder" display board (on which the children can use cards to make up "silly sentences"), Elise found that Arief was able to concentrate on the activity and to interact with a few other children who had become intrigued by his expertise. These kinds of simple environmental changes can set the stage for greater engagement and success for children with disabilities in inclusive environments (Sandall & Schwartz, 2002).

The physical environment may also contribute to self-regulation, when it is set up so that children can function independently in choosing activities, taking materials out, using them appropriately, and putting them back. Most early childhood programs value the development of independence and self-regulation, and some curricula, such as Montessori (Torrence & Chattin-McNichols, 2000) and Tools of the Mind (Bodrova & Leong, 2007), pay great attention to the physical environment as a tool in developing self-regulation. Elise's classroom is a good example; she notes that as compared with last year (when she was constantly being asked for materials by the children), this year's reorganized environment makes it easy for children to find their own supplies, get books to read, return their clipboards to the right place, and so on.

Establishing Routines and Schedules

As noted in Figure 7.1, when teachers establish clear routines and a predictable environment early in the year, children are able to be more focused, persistent, and self-regulated. A dependable classroom structure frees children to concentrate on their activities without worrying about arbitrary interruptions or unexpected changes in the routine. The training manual for Tools of the Mind advises staff to invest a great deal of time in establishing such routines early in the year. Elise is seeing the payoff now, when the children are able to continue the routines even when they have a substitute teacher, reminding the sub that "We always start our group meeting with a song and the 'freeze game.'"

It is also important to have enough time for children to become fully involved in whatever it is that they are learning, whether in an art experience, dramatic play, a new project, or a science exploration. As children get older, such activities can extend not only for longer periods of time during the day but also over several days or even weeks—as long as the schedule has been designed to support this. Because her program values the deep engagement of children in pretend play, Elise's schedule has a long time block for children to plan, dramatize, and re-dramatize the stories that they have been reading.

Making the Most of Small Groups

Children usually learn more and function better in small groups than in whole-group activities. It is not surprising that many early childhood curricula, and guidelines for program practices, recommend intentional and extensive use of small-group times.

Small-group times may take many forms, depending on the specifics of the curriculum and the developmental and educational needs of the children (Graves, 1997). Some curricula (e.g., High/Scope and Tools of the Mind) emphasize planned, teacher-facilitated small-group times as a formal part of the daily schedule.

Why do small groups seem to work so well—for people of all ages? People process information better and seem to stay more attentive, focused, and engaged when they are part of a small group in which everyone has a chance to contribute and to hear what others think (Marzano, 2007). Even nonverbal children are able to observe others' work in a small group and get ideas from their peers. Young children seem to find it easier to regulate their feelings and behavior when fewer children are present and when the teacher can more easily scaffold their self-regulation. Relationships are strengthened in small groups: Teachers find it easier to get to know children in smaller groups and to individualize their interactions and feedback depending on what they observe.

If teachers gradually implement small-group work, children can participate productively in small groups even when a teacher is not present. In Tools of the

Mind classrooms like Elise's kindergarten, one often sees children working in small, collaborative groups, helping each other as "study buddies" or working persistently and independently with occasional help from other group members. Similarly, in Reggio Emilia programs children often engage in rich peer-group discussions without teacher direction, for example, deciding on how to proceed with some aspect of the work on a project (Project Zero & Reggio Children, 2001).

All of these variations on small-group work need careful thought and planning. Figure 7.2 offers suggestions to get started.

❧ FIGURE 7.2   Nuts and Bolts: Making the Most of Teacher-Facilitated Small-Group Times

Small-group times offer many opportunities to strengthen children's positive approaches to learning: their interest, pleasure, motivation to learn, attention, persistence, flexibility, and self-regulation. However, teachers who have not regularly used small groups may need support in making the most of these times in the schedule. Following are suggestions drawn from several resources:

◆ Consider options—whether to have all of the children in small groups at the same time, with the teacher rotating among them, or whether to work intensively with one small group while other children are involved in worthwhile independent activities that need minimal supervision. In either case, staffing needs to be considered. Are there volunteers who can help?

◆ Have clear goals in mind for the small-group times—emphasizing enthusiasm and engagement as goals but also incorporating other goals related to curriculum outcomes or standards.

◆ Start slowly (brief small-group times with simple materials)

◆ Don't feel that there needs to be something new for small-group time every day. Sometimes revisiting familiar play materials ("what else can we build with the Legos?") will result in a high level of engagement and flexible, inventive use of materials.

◆ Help children learn the small-group routine by practicing it repeatedly and using physical prompts such as name cards.

◆ Sit beside a child who is unfocused or discouraged and provide physical, verbal, or emotional support that leads to success. Alternate taking the lead with the child if necessary.

◆ Encourage children to help each other, thereby increasing their interest and pleasure in the activity, as well as their motivation.

◆ Select materials that reflect children's interests and that can be used in different ways depending on interests, abilities, and culture.

◆ When working directly with the small group, make it a priority to foster high levels of engagement by every child (this is easier than in a large group). Look at, talk with, prompt, and affirm each child's contributions.

◆ Especially if children have disabilities, make sure each child can meaningfully participate in the activity. Adapt materials and procedures as necessary, either in advance or as you see the need during the small-group time.

TOOL 2: SPECIFIC TEACHING PRACTICES

Whether early childhood educators are working with infants, toddlers, preschoolers, or kindergarten–primary-grade children, and in whatever kind of setting, they have almost limitless opportunities to teach in ways that build children's positive approaches to learning. This section will describe and give examples of only four such practices: modeling positive approaches to learning, emphasizing learning goals, scaffolding and elaborating on children's ideas and actions, and offering meaningful and challenging choices. These are not unusual practices—they are commonly used in high quality early childhood education—but when they are implemented intentionally they have great potential to increase children's enthusiasm and engagement.

Modeling Positive Approaches to Learning

Teachers and others who work in early childhood programs have tremendous power to influence children's feelings and behavior through modeling the attitudes and behaviors they wish children to adopt.

What are good opportunities to do this? Sometimes it might be in a class meeting (such as those described in Chapter 5) in which the teacher is introducing a new project or activity. Other, more informal occasions for modeling are also available to a teacher. For example, Elise was genuinely fascinated with the caterpillars that were sent for the kindergarten class to observe, and the children could see her curiosity. They were also able to observe Elise's patience in waiting for a caterpillar to climb up the side of the box. Because of their close relationships with Elise, the children are likely to practice those behaviors.

Teachers also model positive approaches to learning when they pay focused attention to what a child or group of children is doing. Elise addressed Eduardo individually, "I know you wanted to show me what you're doing, Eduardo. Now I have time to see how you're using the magnifying glass to watch the caterpillars. How about if I sit right here and watch how you do it?"

Emphasizing the Goals of Learning and Mastery

Why do children want to participate in certain tasks? Children may be oriented toward either (1) achieving competence or mastery while enjoying the task, exerting effort, and wanting to learn (*learning goals*) or (2) achieving correct performance to receive praise and recognition or to avoid looking stupid (*performance goals*) (Dweck, 2000; Wigfield & Eccles, 2002). But children aren't just born either learning-goal-oriented or performance-goal-oriented. Rather, they develop these orientations as a result of family and school influences. To support positive approaches to learning, including motivation to learn, we want to help children to focus more on learning goals.

The children in Elise's kindergarten seem highly motivated to become involved in the class caterpillar project. When introducing this project and in the daily discussions she has with the children, Elise deliberately emphasizes learning goals. Learning goals encourage children to become involved in the activities because they are curious about how caterpillars live, eat, and turn into butterflies, and because they want to become more capable at tasks such as making illustrated booklets for the preschoolers down the hall to enjoy. Because Elise has emphasized learning goals in this project and throughout the year, the children seem motivated not by a desire to get 10 stars on a chart for completing the 10 project activities, but by their interest in mastering important skills (such as using a magnifying glass or writing down observations in a notebook) and by the satisfaction of learning something new and challenging.

Elaborating on and Scaffolding Children's Ideas and Actions

When teachers elaborate on and scaffold what children say and do, they are promoting the approaches to learning that can lead to greater learning and achievement. In a series of studies of engagement (de Kruif et al., 2000; McWilliam, Scarborough, & Kim, 2003), the most engaged children were in classrooms with teachers whom the researchers called "elaborative." These teachers were frequently expanding on what the children were already doing, praising the children's work, and getting children who weren't engaged to participate in new activities. Interestingly (and linking back to Chapter 5 on relationships), these same teachers were rated especially high on the emotional quality of their interactions with the children.

This description of elaboration is typical of what Elise does in her kindergarten classroom. For example, when she joined quiet Eduardo as he was using the magnifying glass, she offered a sort of play-by-play accompaniment: "Oh, I see one of the caterpillars crawling onto a leaf. There he goes! Oops, he almost fell off, but he's back on the leaf again. Do you see him, too? I wonder what would happen if you moved the magnifying glass closer. Can you see better now?" Eduardo's smiles, nods, and actions showed that he was connecting with and responding to Elise's elaborations.

Elise also practices scaffolding, a tool with great power to promote children's motivation to learn and their self-regulation. A teacher or other adult scaffolds or supports a child's performance by initially providing assistance needed for success (e.g., helping the child count a group of objects, or doing part of a jigsaw puzzle for the child). As the child becomes able to do the task independently, the adult gradually removes the assistance.

The Vygotskian-influenced Tools of the Mind curriculum (Bodrova & Leong, 2007) helps teachers to intentionally consider what scaffolds children may need, when, and for what—at different times of the year, for different kinds of activities, or for children with different learning needs or styles. Sometimes Elise's physical presence is all that is needed to help the children attend and persist in their work. Elise also scaffolds children's learning when she sits at a table and helps just enough with a challenging task to allow children to complete it successfully. The goal is not only to create successful outcomes for children but to support the continuing motivation to learn that comes with successful performance.

Simple "mediators" are also very helpful in the scaffolding process. In Elise's classroom, many of these mediators are physical (e.g., the children listening to a story tape of *The Very Hungry Caterpillar* have clipboards with pictorial reminders, prompting them to draw or write their answers to certain questions). If pairs of children are doing an activity such as "sharing their weekend news," they use cardboard ears and lips to remind themselves whose turn it is to be the speaker and who is the listener—thereby encouraging their self-regulation, focused attention, and persistence. As children internalize and master the techniques of listening to one another and taking turns, these concrete props can be removed.

Although these examples are drawn from one kindergarten curriculum, the general strategy may be used with a variety of curriculum models, and with children of differing ages, cultures, and experiences. Often the only thing a child needs in order to become deeply and enthusiastically engaged in a learning activity is the supportive presence of a caring teacher who gives just enough help and encouragement to keep the learning going.

Offering Meaningful, Challenging Choices

Although it is organized and clearly structured, Elise's kindergarten classroom is full of choices, and the children seem to flourish in this environment. From early childhood through adolescence and beyond, learners are likely to become more interested and involved when they have choices as to what and how they will learn (Brophy, 2004; Kohn, 1993).

This does not mean that everything has to be a choice, or that any old choice will do. But knowing the power of choices in supporting positive approaches to learning, early childhood educators may think about ways to increase both the number and the quality of choices available.

When everyone has to do the same thing at the same time and at the same pace, it's not surprising that children—especially those who learn in different ways and at a different pace—may either rebel or disengage. In other classrooms the problem may be that there are too many choices, with no encouragement for children to persist in the choices they make and to become more deeply engaged. In those environments, children may flit from one superficially appealing choice to another, with little learning going on, and with little opportunity to become not only motivated but also persistent and self-regulated.

If choices are to be effective tools in promoting positive approaches to learning, they must be meaningful and challenging. As explained in Chapter 6, in Tools of the Mind preschools each child makes a daily "play plan," first deciding what to play, and drawing and writing a simple representation of the plan before moving into an extended pretend play period. When children get older (like Elise's kindergartners), the plan becomes more fully developed and extends over a longer period of time, taking the form of a child's individual "learning plan," again with choices available.

WHEN MORE INTENTIONAL STRATEGIES MAY BE NEEDED

The teaching practices we have reviewed will help all children build their enthusiasm and engagement in learning. However, a teacher's use of some additional strategies may be needed for children who have challenging behaviors or who begin school already discouraged and disengaged.

Removing the Barriers Presented by Children's Challenging Behavior

When children (either individual children or the whole group) are spending much of their time in conflicts, arguments, angry outbursts, and disruptive behavior, there is little opportunity for them to experience and practice enthusiastic, engaged learning. Indeed, we see a negative spiral: Children are disruptive, teachers respond negatively, children's disruption escalates and spreads to more children, and the environment becomes less and less nurturing and engaging for children and teachers alike. Both joy and learning suffer.

Many of the strategies already discussed will prevent challenging behaviors from occurring in the first place. But there still may be children whose intense anger or other challenges persist. Some of these children may have disabilities, and others may be responding to stresses in their family or community. In any case, the challenging behavior must be constructively addressed so that these children, too, may feel the pleasure of being enthusiastic and engaged in learning.

Resources such as those from the Center on the Social and Emotional Foundations for Early Learning (CSEFEL) will help address these issues (http://www .vanderbilt.edu/csefel). To assist teachers in working constructively to prevent and address challenging behavior, the Center has proposed the "pyramid model" shown in Figure 7.3 as their conceptual framework (Center on the Social and Emotional Foundations for Early Learning, 2008). At the most basic level, personnel and policies are needed to support the implementation of these practices. The foundation of the pyramid is nurturing, responsive relationships with children and families (the focus of Chapter 5), and at the next level is the task of creating supportive environments for all children (the focus of this chapter). These will prevent or reduce misbehavior for most children. Working up the levels of the pyramid, teachers may implement specific social and emotional teaching strategies. For example, some children may need a private corner to help them persist at their work; others may need a pictorial schedule to help them predict what will happen next, thus allowing them to stay focused and engaged. For those few children whose behavior presents continuing challenges even in a supportive environment, targeted and intensive interventions—including referrals to special services—may be needed. Resources from CSEFEL and others (e.g., Fox, Dunlap, Hemmeter, Joseph, & Strain, 2003; Kaiser & Rasminsky, 2003; Sandall & Schwartz, 2002) can supplement these few examples.

The important thing to keep in mind is that all children—including those who exhibit challenging behaviors—can be helped to become more engaged, motivated, and happy about learning.

FIGURE 7.3   A Pyramid Model for Supporting Social and Emotional Competence in Infants and Young Children

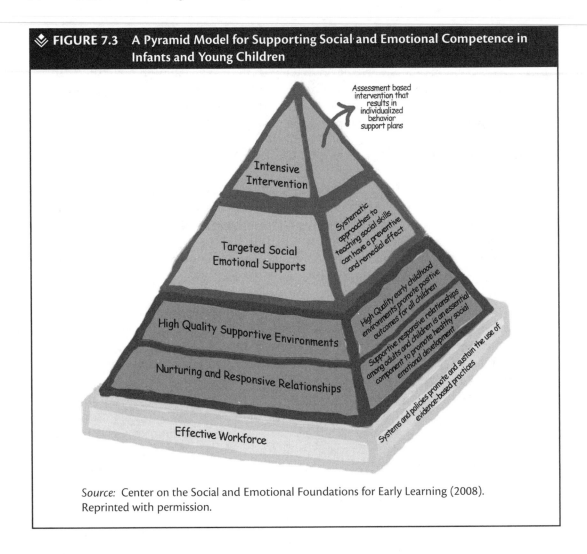

Source: Center on the Social and Emotional Foundations for Early Learning (2008). Reprinted with permission.

Helping Children Already Discouraged and Disengaged

As with children who have challenging behaviors, there may be other children who come into the classroom already seemingly uninterested and defeatist about their own abilities. As discussed in Chapter 4, there may be many reasons for this level of discouragement and disengagement. Fortunately, relatively few children in the early years show such discouragement, as compared with adolescents (National Research Council, 2003). But those few should be of great concern so that their downward spiral may be reversed.

The first step is to build or rebuild a relationship with the discouraged and disengaged child. Sometimes these children are simply not appealing to teachers, who then may avoid interacting with the very children who need those relationships the most. Intentionally investing one-on-one time each day is essential. As noted in Chapter 5, even a few minutes a day can make a big difference. In this time, a teacher can simply learn more about a child, being with him in a friendly way that makes no demands but simply shows liking and interest. A good time for such "close encounters," is often early in the morning, or perhaps snack time or lunch time. As the relationship grows, discouraged and disengaged children may spontaneously begin to participate in activities; teachers may also connect them with other, less discouraged children in partner or buddy situations. Offering activities at which discouraged children can succeed builds confidence so that they may be more willing to tackle potentially frustrating learning activities.

LOOKING BACK AND LOOKING FORWARD

The last three chapters have described tools for supporting children's enthusiasm and engagement through relationships (Chapter 5), curriculum (Chapter 6), and environments and teaching strategies (Chapter 7). Although discussed in separate chapters, these areas are connected and support one another (e.g., even the most promising curriculum will be ineffective if teachers' relationships with children are negative). In Chapter 8 we will see how children's enthusiasm and engagement can be assessed in ways that will inform teachers' decisions about how best to promote these essential approaches to learning.

 Reflection, Discussion, and Action

1. In your own program or one in which you are observing, make a diagram of the indoor or outdoor physical environment. Keeping in mind the goal of increasing children's engagement, you might identify changes in the physical environment that would be helpful either for the whole group or for certain children. If possible, implement the changes and observe the effects.

2. Select one of the teaching strategies described in this chapter (e.g., being more focused on learning goals) and make a personal action plan to use this strategy more intentionally. You might keep a journal of your experiences with this new or enhanced strategy. What is easy about doing this, and what is difficult? Do be sure to give yourself and the children time to become comfortable with the strategy. What results do you see?

3. Identify one child for thoughtfully targeted intervention. This might be a child whose enthusiasm and engagement are being undermined because of persistent challenging behaviors, or perhaps a child who is especially discouraged and disengaged. Using some of the suggestions in this chapter, make a plan for this child, implement it over time, and note the results.

8 Tools to Assess Children's Approaches to Learning

Martha is a first-year teacher in an urban first grade. She and Jeff, a student teacher, are meeting after school to discuss a project about trees, which they will begin this week. The district's curriculum requires that this project be science-focused, with an emphasis on several of the state science standards. However, Martha also wants to use the project to strengthen the children's motivation to learn, their persistence, and their ability to plan and carry out their plans.

During their meeting, Martha and Jeff talk about what they have observed so far about these components of approaches to learning, both in the class as a whole and in the behavior of individual children. Looking forward to how the project may unfold, Martha and Jeff consider ways that they will systematically gather and use information about how their first-graders are learning, as well as what they are learning.

CONTINUOUS, THOUGHTFUL ASSESSMENT has become a key feature of quality early childhood education, increasing the likelihood of positive outcomes for children (Hyson et al., 2006). I will begin this chapter with a review of some general principles of appropriate, effective assessment. Then I will introduce three tools that can help educators use assessment to support positive approaches to learning: (1) new ways to use comprehensive assessment systems; (2) specialized approaches-to-learning assessments; and (3) a systematic plan to use the results of these assessments. The chapter ends with recommendations for reducing the risks and maximizing the potential of assessing children's approaches to learning.

 Goals of This Chapter

After reading this chapter, you will be better able to

1. Apply the general principles of appropriate, effective assessment when assessing children's approaches to learning.

2. Select appropriate classroom-based assessments of children's approaches to learning.

3. Describe the new directions researchers are taking in assessing approaches to learning.

4. Use assessment results to create environments that promote positive approaches to learning for all children.

5. Take steps to reduce the risks and increase the potential of assessing children's enthusiasm and engagement.

GOOD EARLY CHILDHOOD ASSESSMENT: A REMINDER OF BASIC PRINCIPLES

When assessing children's enthusiasm and engagement, the same principles should apply as when assessing any other aspect of development and learning. In a joint position statement, NAEYC and NAECS/SDE (2003) made specific, evidence-based recommendations concerning early childhood assessment. Summarized in Figure 8.1, these recommendations remind us that—no matter what else—the primary goal of early childhood assessment is to benefit children.

Several aspects of these recommendations should receive special emphasis when we think about assessing young children's approaches to learning. As emphasized in the position statement's recommendations and indicators, assessments must use *multiple sources of evidence*. No one source of evidence can lead to definitive conclusions about a child's current level of enthusiasm for and engagement in learning.

❖ **FIGURE 8.1   Research Reminder: Appropriate, Effective Assessment in Early Childhood Education**

- ❖ *Recommendation.* Make ethical, appropriate, valid and reliable assessment a central part of all early childhood programs. To assess young children's strengths, progress, and needs, use assessment methods that are developmentally appropriate, culturally and linguistically responsive, tied to children's daily activities, supported by professional development, inclusive of families, and connected to specific, beneficial purposes: (1) making sound decisions about teaching and learning, (2) identifying significant concerns that may require focused intervention for individual children, and (3) helping programs improve their educational and developmental interventions.

- ❖ *Indicators of effective assessment practices*
  - Ethical principles guide assessment practices.
  - Assessment instruments are used for their intended purposes.
  - Assessments are appropriate for ages and other characteristics of children being assessed.
  - Assessment instruments are in compliance with professional criteria for quality.
  - What is assessed is developmentally and educationally significant.
  - Assessment evidence is used to understand and improve learning.
  - Assessment evidence is gathered from realistic settings and situations that reflect children's actual performance.
  - Assessments use multiple sources of evidence gathered over time.
  - Screening is always linked to follow-up.
  - Use of individually administered, norm-referenced tests is limited.
  - Staff and families are knowledgeable about assessment.

Source: NAEYC & NAECS/SDE (2003, pp. 2–3).

The full NAEYC and NAECS/SDE 2003 position statement "Early Childhood Curriculum, Assessment, and Program Evaluation—Building an Effective, Accountable System in Programs for Children Birth Through Age 8" is available online at http://www.naeyc.org/about/positions/pdf/CAPEexpand.pdf

Two examples from Martha's first-grade class illustrate this point. Isabel, who with her family recently emigrated from Central America, seemed reluctant to participate in the classroom. When Martha made a home visit, though, she saw that rather than being unmotivated, Isabel was curious and intensely involved in familiar activities. Similarly, when Martha used a formal paper-and-pencil assessment of the children's persistence, Leonard performed poorly; however, when Martha and Jeff watched Leonard working with the construction materials that he loves, he seemed unusually persistent and focused.

A second key point from the NAEYC and NAECS/SDE recommendations has to do with the *purposes of assessment*. Although assessment has many purposes, the most important goal—prominently featured in the position statement's recommendations and indicators—is to help teachers make "sound decisions about teaching and learning": that is, to provide the kind of information that will be useful in planning curriculum and teaching methods for a group and for individual children. In the case of assessments of children's approaches to learning, it is especially important to keep this purpose in mind. Assessment results should not be used to label some children as innately unmotivated. The evidence is clear that children's positive approaches to learning can be significantly improved through good early childhood experiences. Therefore, assessment of children's approaches to learning should be a guide to action, with the results helping teachers plan curriculum and teaching methods to support all children's progress. With these principles in mind, let's look now at various ways to assess children's enthusiasm and engagement.

TOOL 1: FAMILIAR ASSESSMENTS USED IN SOME NEW WAYS

Many early childhood programs use or are planning to adopt a comprehensive instrument with which they regularly assess children's progress in many aspects of development and learning. Fortunately, quite a few of these assessments have scales or sets of items that are related to what we call approaches to learning, although they may not use the same terminology. This section will describe three examples of such assessments: two that are linked to specific curriculum models and another that is not.

The Child Observation Record

The first example is the Child Observation Record (COR), which was developed to accompany the High/Scope curriculum described in Chapter 6. However, a number of programs that follow other curricula also use the COR as their comprehensive assessment.

Briefly, with the COR the teacher, or someone else who has been trained to use the instrument, assesses each child's behavior and activities in six categories: (1) initiative, (2) social relations, (3) creative representation, (4) music and movement, (5) language and literacy, and (6) logic and mathematics. (The Infant/Toddler version of the COR has somewhat different categories.) Over several months, the teacher writes short descriptions of children's behavior in each of these areas during typical daily routines. Several times a year, the teacher then uses these notes to rate each child's behavior on specific items within each category, using a 1–5 numerical scale ranging from simpler to more complex developmental levels. Programs can use this information to help track children's progress, strengths, and needs over time; to plan instruction; and to communicate with families.

Within this assessment system, the category of "Initiative" (called "Sense of Self" in the Infant/Toddler version) most closely parallels aspects of approaches to learning. As assessed in the COR, initiative is the child's ability to begin and follow through on tasks. Initiative also refers to the child's ability to make and carry out choices, decisions, and plans; to solve problems using materials; and to coordinate their ideas and actions with others (High/Scope Educational Research Foundation, 2003). The COR's category of "Social Relations" also includes some items relevant to approaches to learning, such as solving inter-personal conflicts, or understanding and expressing feelings, both of which are aspects of self-regulation.

Creative Curriculum's Developmental Continuum Assessment

The Creative Curriculum (Dodge et al., 2002) was also discussed in Chapter 6. Like High/Scope and its COR, the Creative Curriculum is accompanied by an assessment system, the Developmental Continuum Assessment, that aligns with the curriculum's objectives. An Assessment Toolkit helps teachers plan for a group of children and individual children. Worksheets help teachers follow children's progress in each of the areas on the continuum, both as a class group and in individual child profiles constructed three times a year. Progress reports summarize findings and help teachers and families make decisions about next steps.

A number of items in the Developmental Continuum are related to approaches to learning, although the Continuum does not have a specific approaches-to-learning category. The area that seems most closely aligned to approaches to learning is found within Cognitive Development, in the category of "Learning and Problem-Solving." These items (with their approaches-to-learning equivalents in italics) include "Observes objects and events with curiosity" (*Interest*), "Approaches problems flexibly, using multiple strategies" (*Flexible problem-solving*), and "Shows persistence in approaching tasks" (*Persistence*).

Additionally, the area of Social and Emotional Development includes these goals and objectives: "Demonstrates self-direction and independence" (*Motivation to learn*), "Takes responsibility for own well-being" (*Self-regulation*), and "Uses thinking skills to resolve conflicts" (*Self-regulation*).

Work Sampling System

Unlike the COR and the Developmental Continuum Assessment, the final example of a "multifunction assessment" was not developed to accompany one curriculum model but has been used with a variety of curricula. Work Sampling (Meisels, Jablon, Marsden, Dichtelmiller, & Dorfman, 2001) is an ongoing class-room performance assessment system based on national and state standards for children's learning and development. It was designed to be used with children from preschool through fifth grade. A related assessment, The Ounce Scale (Meisels, Marsden, Dombro, Weston, & Jewkes, 2003) uses a similar approach to assessing children from birth to age 3. In Work Sampling, teachers use developmental checklists, portfolios, and summary reports to chart progress in seven areas: personal and social development, language and literacy, mathematical thinking, scientific thinking, social studies, the arts, and physical development and health. As these assessments are done throughout the year, they may be used to help teachers plan learning activities that support development.

The "Personal and Social Development" domain of Work Sampling has a section specifically called "Approaches to Learning." The items are very similar to the way in which the National Education Goals Panel described the approaches-to-learning dimension of school readiness. Teachers assess each child on items such as "Shows eagerness and curiosity as a learner," "Sustains attention to a task over a period of time even after encountering problems," and "Approaches tasks with flexibility and inventiveness" (Meisels et al., 2001, pp. 2–3).

As with other areas in Work Sampling, teachers consider the evidence they have gathered in authentic classroom settings to summarize the child's progress on a three-level scale: "not yet," "in process," or "proficient."

Common Elements in Multifunction-Assessment Examples

These three widely used assessment systems illustrate how multifunction assessments may include aspects of approaches to learning. The examples have some interesting similarities:

* Each begins with teachers' observations of children's behavior in ordinary, authentic classroom activities.
* Each encourages teachers to use those observations and other evidence to arrive at summary ratings.
* Each system assesses children at multiple points during the year.
* Each system emphasizes that results should be used to create greater understanding and better teaching of young children.

These common elements are consistent with the assessment principles described in the joint position statement of NAEYC and NAECS/SDE (2003).

Figure 8.2 summarizes the key features of these and two other multifunction assessments and provides Web-based and other references for more information. All are potentially useful sources of insight about children's enthusiasm and engagement; other systems not described in this chapter may also be used for this purpose.

Reviewing Your Program's Assessment System

In Martha's school district, there is a comprehensive assessment system in place, but the system does not include assessment of approaches to learning. If your program has already adopted a comprehensive assessment system, it will be important to look at it from the perspective of approaches to learning:

❧ FIGURE 8.2   Nuts and Bolts: Approaches to Learning in Commonly Used "Multifunction" Assessment Systems

◆ *Child Observation Record (COR).* Aligns with High/Scope curriculum. Teacher observations and anecdotal records are followed by ratings in six developmental areas. Items in the category of "Initiative" tap children's flexible problem-solving, focused attention, and persistence. An online option is available.

    For more information: High/Scope Educational Research Foundation (2003); http://www.highscope.org/Content.asp?ContentId=63

◆ *Developmental Continuum.* Aligns with the Creative Curriculum. Teachers observe children and use worksheets to record progress and profiles for class and individual children. Items in areas of Cognitive Development and Social and Emotional Development parallel aspects of approaches to learning, including persistence, initiative, motivation to learn, and self-regulation. An online option is available.

    For more information: http://www.teachingstrategies.com/page/CA_AssessmentSolutions.cfm

◆ *Devereux Early Childhood Assessment (DECA).* Strengths-based assessment of children ages 2–5, completed by teachers and parents. After a period of first-hand observation, the teacher and parent rate the child on how often he or she shows each of 27 positive behaviors. Items that are closely related to dimensions and components of approaches to learning include "chooses to do tasks that are challenging for him/her" and "shows patience."

    For more information: LeBuffe & Naglieri (1999); http://www.devereuxearlychildhood.org

◆ *Galileo.* Computer-based assessment tool that tracks children's progress in a number of school readiness areas, including approaches to learning. Assessment relies on teachers' direct observations, anecdotal narratives, samples of children's work, and family input.

    For more information: http://www.ati-online.com

◆ *Work Sampling.* An ongoing classroom performance assessment system. Teachers use developmental checklists, portfolios, and summary reports to chart progress in seven areas. The Personal and Social Development domain has a section called Approaches to Learning, including items related to eagerness and curiosity, attention and persistence, and flexibility and inventiveness.

    For more information: Meisels et al. (2001); http://phcatalog.pearson.com/program_multiple.cfm?site_id=1021&discipline_id=3361&subarea_id=0&program_id=941

  ♦ Does the assessment include items that tap the dimensions and compo-
    nents of enthusiasm and engagement?
  ♦ Are there missing pieces?
  ♦ If so, and if you believe these should be assessed, might it be possible to
    supplement this assessment instrument in some way?

With the help of her university mentor, Martha has added items that will give
her useful information about her children's enthusiasm and engagement, even
though these items are not part of the district's assessment system.

TOOL 2: SPECIALIZED ASSESSMENTS OF APPROACHES TO LEARNING

In addition to multifunction assessments, some assessments are specifically
designed to gather information about aspects of children's approaches to learning. As we will see, a few of these have been designed for use by teachers, while
other assessments have been designed for use by researchers. It is helpful to know
about both.

Assessments for Use by Classroom Teachers

Two examples will be described in this section: The first is a simple tool that
teachers can use to assess the engagement of individual children during daily
routines. The second instrument allows teachers to gather information about a
wide range of learning behaviors or approaches to learning. Figure 8.3 summarizes information about these and two other potential assessment tools for classroom use.

Scale for Teachers' Assessment of Routines Engagement. To help teachers keep
track of children's engagement during classroom routines, Casey and McWilliam
(2007) developed the Scale for Teachers' Assessment of Routines Engagement
(STARE). This simple instrument is appropriate for use with typically developing
children and with children who have disabilities. To use the instrument, teachers
observe a child for about 10 minutes in routines such as arrival, group time, free
play, teacher-directed activities, lunch, and outside time. During each routine, an
observer uses a form to note whether the child is engaged with adults, peers,
and/or materials—ranging from almost none of the time to almost all of the time.
Additionally, the teacher notes the *level* of the child's engagement, ranging from
Nonengagement ("inappropriate behavior; zoning out") through Sophisticated
Engagement ("symbolic talk, pretending, persisting"). The information allows the
teacher to learn more about a child's patterns of engagement, which can help the
teacher modify instruction or develop specific interventions.

❧ FIGURE 8.3   Nuts and Bolts: Specialized Assessments of Approaches to Learning for Use by Classroom Teachers

◆ *ECLS-K Approaches to Learning Assessment.* The Early Childhood Longitudinal Study—Kindergarten (ECLS-K) assesses children's approaches to learning at kindergarten entry using parent and teacher ratings. Items focus on children's attentiveness, persistence, eagerness to learn, independence in learning, flexibility, and organization in approaching learning tasks. The scale is an adaptation of sections of the Social Skills Rating System (SSRS) (Gresham & Elliott, 1990).

   For more information: National Center for Education Statistics (n.d.); http://nces.ed.gov/ecls

◆ *Engagement Check II.* This is a simple procedure that teachers can use to determine the extent of group engagement. Teachers count the number of children in the room or group; then they count how many of these children are not engaged. Repeated quick observations give an average percentage of engaged children.

   For more information: McWilliam (1998); http://www.vanderbiltchildrens.com/interior.php?mid=1177

◆ *Learning-to-Learn Scales (LTLS).* A teacher thinks about a child's behavior over the past two months and categorizes each of the scales' items as "Most often applies" to this child, "Sometimes applies," or "Doesn't apply." Items group into six factors: Strategic Planning, Effectiveness Motivation, Interpersonal Responsiveness in Learning, Attention/Concentration, Vocal Engagement in Learning, and Risk Acceptance.

   For more information: Fantuzzo & McDermott (2008); McDermott et al. (2002); Rouse & Fantuzzo (2008).

◆ *Scale for Teachers' Assessment of Routines Engagement (STARE).* Teachers rate children's amount and level of engagement during classroom routines such as arrival, group time, centers, lunch, and outdoor time.

   For more information: Casey & McWilliam (2007); http://www.fpg.unc.edu/~inclusion/Instruments/STARE/body_stare.htm

---

Learning-to-Learn Scales. A second assessment tool that will soon be available for classroom teachers' use is the Learning-to-Learn Scales (LTLS) (Fantuzzo & McDermott, 2008), which is based on the earlier Preschool Learning Behaviors Scale developed for use in research by McDermott and colleagues (McDermott, Leigh, & Perry, 2002). Once the validation research is completed, this measure may be used to learn more about children, to help teachers self-assess, and to inform decisions about how to enhance positive approaches to learning in the preschool classroom.

With this measure, a teacher thinks about a child's behavior over the past two months and categorizes each item as "Most often applies" to this child,

"Sometimes applies," or "Doesn't apply." Teacher responses give information about six aspects of children's learning behaviors: Strategic Planning (an example behavior: "Develops plan after considering possible consequences"), Effectiveness Motivation ("Engages in activity previously found challenging"), Interpersonal Responsiveness in Learning ("Responds positively to suggestions for alternative approaches"), Attention/Concentration ("Remains focused on individual activity for at least 30 minutes"), Vocal Engagement in Learning ("Asks questions and shares ideas"), and Risk Acceptance ("Willingly participates in unfamiliar activities"). The LTLS is designed particularly to detect and differentiate improvements in learning behavior as they emerge over relatively short time intervals.

Assessments for Use by Researchers

This section includes examples of assessments of aspects of approaches to learning that are designed for use by researchers. Two additional examples of research assessment instruments are included in the summary in Figure 8.4. For all early childhood professionals, these kinds of assessments will provide useful information about the predictors and effects of children's self-regulation, flexible problem solving, and other approaches-to-learning components.

Touch Your Toes! A Behavioral Measure of Preschool Self-Regulation. One new assessment of children's self-regulation is called "Touch Your Toes!" (Cameron et al., in press). To conduct this assessment, a trained assessor invites individual children to play a game. The assessor gives the child a series of directions such as "Touch your head" or "Touch your toes," but with the complication of switching the rules: After a series of appropriate responses, the child is then asked to respond in the opposite way—touching their head when the command is to touch their toes. Children who were better able to use "inhibitory control" in this task were more likely to score better on emergent literacy, vocabulary, and math skills (McClelland et al., 2007).

Problem-Solving Flexibility Task. Another relatively new measure is designed to assess children's flexibility in problem-solving, another important aspect of approaches to learning (George & Greenfield, 2005). In George and Greenfield's study, children were asked to choose the "odd" item (Which one is different?) from three choices (e.g., in one set of clown pictures, one of the clowns was not wearing a hat). A series of such problems were given to the child. To get the right answers, the child had to switch her or his problem-solving strategies each time (e.g., perhaps the next set of three pictures had two pictures of clowns and one of a monkey). Children who performed better on these tasks used more flexible strategies to solve the problems, rather than getting stuck on the first approach they used.

❧ **FIGURE 8.4**   **Nuts and Bolts: Specialized Assessments of Approaches to Learning for Use by Researchers**

- ◆ *Children's Academic Intrinsic Motivation Inventory (CAIMI).* Parents complete this measure by responding to a series of statements about their child. The measure assesses characteristics such as children's enjoyment of learning, mastery orientation, persistence, curiosity, and involvement in challenging tasks. Versions are available for older and younger children (Y-CAIMI).
    For more information: Gottfried, Fleming, & Gottfried (1998).

- ◆ *Children's Continuous Performance Test (CPT).* A computerized measure of young children's ability to pay attention, an ability that is an important component of approaches to learning and of "executive function." Younger children and children who have been diagnosed with attention deficits perform significantly worse on this assessment than older or typically developing children.
    For more information: Blair, Zelazo, & Greenberg (2005); Mahone, Pillion, Hoffman, Hiemenz, & Denckla (2005).

- ◆ *Problem-Solving Flexibility Task.* Individual children are asked to figure out which of three pictures is different. Each set of pictures in the series requires them to use a different rule or problem-solving strategy.
    For more information: George & Greenfield (2005).

- ◆ *Touch Your Toes! A Behavioral Measure of Preschool Self-Regulation.* Individual children are given a simple, gamelike test of following directions. Scores reflect children's self-regulatory abilities.
    For more information: Cameron et al. (in press).

TOOL 3: A PLAN TO USE THE RESULTS

As we see from these examples, more and more resources are available to help teachers and researchers assess young children's approaches to learning. This is surely a good thing. However, assessment is not an end in itself but a means to an end. The best assessment strategies are useless unless there is a process to *use* the results systematically and effectively. Figure 8.5 may help practitioners think about this process. The figure presents a five-stage model of what has been called a "Documentation and Assessment Cycle."

As they cycle through the five stages in this model, teachers "identify learning goals, collect evidence, describe and analyze the evidence, interpret results in light of learning goals, and apply this information to future planning" (Hyson et al., 2006, p. 28). This cycle is similar to the process teachers go through when they engage in action research within their classrooms (Falk & Blumenreich, 2005; Sagor, 2004).

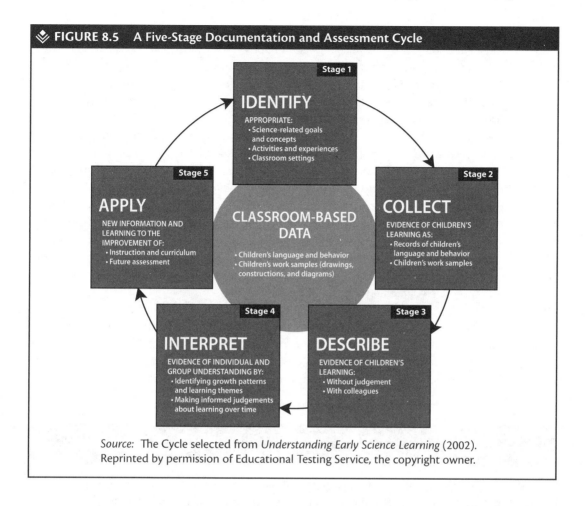

FIGURE 8.5   A Five-Stage Documentation and Assessment Cycle

Source: The Cycle selected from *Understanding Early Science Learning* (2002). Reprinted by permission of Educational Testing Service, the copyright owner.

The following example with Martha, whom we met in the opening vignette, illustrates how this planning process could work for the assessment of children's approaches to learning:

Martha has a strong commitment to promoting positive approaches to learning, with clear goals for children's enthusiasm and engagement, and with classroom experiences and environments designed to reach these goals. During the year, Martha plans to use many of the assessment methods we have discussed, supplementing the multifunction assessment required by her program with a specialized assessment tool focused just on approaches to learning. In the Trees Project but also in other areas of her program, Martha intends to collect this information from multiple sources (direct observations in different contexts, samples of children's work, and discussions with families) and at multiple times during the year.

Martha uses the information to guide her teaching. For her and for many other early childhood educators, this is the primary purpose of assessment. Early in the year, for example, she learned a great deal from asking her student teacher, Jeff, to do quick observations of children's engagement during class meetings. Martha had learned about class meetings during her teacher preparation program, but once in her own classroom she found that her excitement about using class meetings (see Chapter 5 for a description) was not matched by that of the children, many of whom seemed disinterested and nonengaged. With the information provided by Jeff's observations, Martha made changes in the length and format of these meetings, with the goal of promoting greater engagement. In fact, Martha decided to have the meetings with only half the class at a time.

Martha used the results of regular assessments of children's initiative (with which she had supplemented the multifunction assessment already used in her program) to identify children who need focused intervention to help them choose and stick with activities. Martha's mentor (Martha is part of a first-year teacher induction program) helped her think about how to integrate these interventions within all the other things she is doing in her class. In particular, Martha focused on one child, Travers. Travers has Down syndrome and has had difficulty initiating exploration and play. By pairing Travers with a typically developing peer, Joey, whose strength is initiative, and by giving them jobs to do together, Martha began successfully to scaffold greater initiative on the part of Travers, and greater persistence and self-regulation on the part of his partner Joey.

These are only some of the ways in which early childhood teachers may make effective use of assessment information related to children's approaches to learning. Figure 8.6 invites you to try to expand assessments in specific content areas (such as, in this case, mathematics). Rather than simply gathering

---

❖ FIGURE 8.6   Enhancing the Everyday: Assessing Approaches to Learning as Part of a Mathematics Curriculum

Assessing children's skills is an everyday part of teaching. Here is an example from a mathematics curriculum; you might consider how the assessment could be broadened to include various components of approaches to learning.

In its mathematics curriculum, Brianna's preschool relies on the Workjobs II Number Activities *collection (Baratta-Lorton, 1978). In one activity, children sit in a group of four at a work mat. Each child may decorate a hat using red and yellow flowers. Each child puts six flowers on the hat in whatever combination they like: For example, Jie-Qi might use five red flowers and one yellow flower, and her friend Amanda might choose three of each color. The children are encouraged to talk about their choices using number language.*

Brianna can learn a good deal about each child's understanding of some number concepts from observing this activity—information that will help her implement the math curriculum. But what might she learn about the children's approaches to learning, at the same time? Using the information in this chapter, consider what components of approaches to learning might be evident during the activity (e.g., differences in children's persistence? interest? self-regulation?), how Brianna might systematically document those behaviors, and what she might learn from the results.

masses of data with no purpose beyond filling out forms and filling up notebooks, systematic plans will ensure that children benefit from the time their teachers spend assessing them.

REDUCING THE RISKS AND MAXIMIZING THE POTENTIAL OF ASSESSING CHILDREN'S APPROACHES TO LEARNING

Martha's story leads us to a concluding discussion of the risks and potential in assessing young children's approaches to learning.

The Risks

Because so many people continue to believe that children's approaches to learning are inborn and unchangeable, we must help teachers and others avoid drawing inaccurate conclusions from assessment information. Whenever teachers gather information about a child's engagement, motivation to learn, or other learning behaviors, the question should not be "How does this information allow us to categorize on this child?" Rather, early childhood educators should ask, "How does this information help us know the child better?" and "How does this information give us clues about what experiences this child needs in order to progress?"

Those assessing children's approaches to learning may also run the risk of mistaking surface behavior for underlying attitudes or feelings. For example, if Martha's student teacher Jeff is observing whether children are attending to a group discussion, he may conclude that they are very attentive simply because most of them are looking at Martha and sitting still. But children as well as adults can seem to be paying attention while thinking about other things or tuning out completely. Children may simply be learning to comply with a rule—"Eyes on the teacher!"—rather than being mentally active. To reduce this risk, teachers need multiple ways of assessing children's levels of engagement, not just where their eyes are directed or where their bodies happen to be.

Finally, assessors may draw mistaken conclusions when they assess the approaches to learning of children from diverse cultures. As in other areas of assessment, culture and language may strongly influence how children respond to assessments (NAEYC, 2005b). As we have seen, children from different cultures may have quite different styles of expressing interest, engagement, motivation to learn, and other components of approaches to learning. The picture of children's enthusiasm and engagement will be inaccurate unless the assessment process and instruments are sensitive to these differences.

The Potential Benefits

As the risks are reduced, the potential benefits of assessing children's approaches to learning begin to be seen. Children benefit, but early childhood educators and families can benefit too, as they learn more about children's enthusiasm and engagement and as they use that information in productive ways.

To sustain those benefits, early childhood programs need to establish an environment in which all staff collaborate in documenting children's progress, sharing insights, and considering how to use the information they are gathering together. In such an environment, everyone is interested in learning more about each child's enthusiasm and engagement (as well as other aspects of development and learning) and using that information to try out and evaluate different teaching strategies. Martha is having a hard time promoting such a culture in her new job, but she has already started to connect with a few other first-grade teachers who've agreed to meet regularly to talk about what they are learning from their increasingly systematic assessments of children's progress.

LOOKING BACK AND LOOKING FORWARD

In this chapter we have looked at what teachers do to assess children's approaches to learning. But families, too, should be part of this collaborative culture of assessment, sharing, planning, and celebrating children's increasingly positive approaches to learning. The next chapter will focus on how families contribute to their children's enthusiasm and engagement, and how early childhood programs can support families in this task.

 Reflection, Discussion, and Action

1. If your program—or one in which you are involved as a student—uses a system to assess children's development and learning, analyze that system from an approaches-to-learning perspective. Are enthusiasm, engagement, and other components assessed in this system? If not, what modifications might you recommend?

2. Try out one or more of the assessment tools described in this chapter, either with a whole class or with one or two children. Consider what new insights you may have as a result.

3. Make a plan to use the results of your assessment to make some changes in a specific activity in your program, so as to create more positive approaches to learning. Share the results with colleagues.

9

Tools That Tap the Power of Families

The teaching teams are beginning to plan a series of early evening parent meetings. In this prekindergarten program, each class has two co-teachers, one fluent in Spanish and one in English. Many teachers have close ties to the local community, which includes immigrants from Mexico and Central America. Dissatisfied with family involvement last year, this year the teachers have decided to do things somewhat differently. For example, the teachers have invited two parents and a grandparent to help them plan the meetings. They have decided to use these meetings to help the families understand that, although it's important for children to learn the foundations of reading and writing, it is at least as important for their children to be motivated and interested in learning and to develop habits such as persistence and self-regulation. The teachers also want to support parents in helping their children in these areas. The teachers and the family representatives on the planning committee have a lot of ideas, but they are still struggling to learn how best to connect with all the families in their program about these critical issues.

N THIS CHAPTER I will highlight the many ways in which early childhood pro-grams can expand families' influence on their children's enthusiasm and engage-ment. Chapter 3 described the circles of influence on approaches to learning in terms of Bronfenbrenner's ecological theory (Bronfenbrenner, 1978). Within Bronfenbrenner's framework and in the work of the Harvard Family Research Project (Weiss, Caspe, & Lopez, 2006), connections between families and schools are one of many interacting systems of support for children's development and learning (Hanson & Lynch, 2003; Powell, 2006; Shonkoff & Phillips, 2000).

Drawing upon evidence of the power of families in young children's lives (see Figure 9.1), early childhood educators can tap into this power with a few simple tools: *relationships, focused conversations,* and *practical ideas.* Respectful, reciprocal *relationships* with families create the foundation. Within such relation-ships, it is possible to engage in rich *conversations* with families about many issues, including those focused on their children's enthusiasm for and engage-ment in learning. These conversations create opportunities for teachers to share evidence-based, *practical ideas* and resources about approaches to learning, while being responsive to families' diverse cultures and circumstances. Together, the tools presented in this chapter should create greater enthusiasm and engagement in all children.

❧ FIGURE 9.1   Research Reminders: Importance of Families for Children's Enthusiasm and Engagement

- "Parents' beliefs and behaviors are critical in setting a climate for children's motiva-tional development" (Wigfield et al., 2006, p. 970).
- Toddlers who are securely attached to their mothers are likely to be more enthusias-tic and persistent in tackling a difficult problem-solving task (Arend et al., 1979); securely attached children also show more self-efficacy and confidence when they enter new, challenging situations (Shonkoff & Phillips, 2000).
- Families that emphasize external rewards and punishments for their children's aca-demic performance tend to have children who are less intrinsically motivated to learn (Gottfried et al., 1994).
- Children's "mastery behaviors" are influenced by their parents' feedback. The parents of more mastery-oriented children—including children with disabilities—are in tune with the child's activities, show positive emotion, and avoid being overly intrusive, directive, or critical (Shonkoff & Phillips, 2000; Turner & Johnson, 2003).
- When the home environment is more stimulating and emotionally supportive, chil-dren's overall well-being is enhanced (Shonkoff & Phillips, 2000).
- Preschool children whose parents read more to them develop both higher motiva-tion to read and higher reading achievement (Wigfield et al., 2006).
- Parents who use a more "democratic" child-rearing approach (giving children choices, not bribing them for good performance) tend to have children whose teachers rate them as more interested in learning and more self-motivated (Grolnick & Ryan, 1989).

Goals of This Chapter

After reading this chapter, you will be better able to

1. Establish strong relationships with all families.

2. Communicate effectively with families about their children's approaches to learning.

3. Draw upon evidence-based practices that families can use to promote enthusiasm and engagement in their children.

TOOL 1: RELATIONSHIPS WITH FAMILIES

After describing the kinds of relationships that are needed, I will outline some specific steps that early childhood educators can take to strengthen those relationships.

Why Should Relationships Be *Reciprocal*?

Just as relationships are the foundation for working with young children (see Chapter 5), relationships are essential to partnering effectively with families (Koralek, 2007). More specifically, relationships play a key role in helping families support their children's enthusiasm for and engagement in learning. In the past, schools and teachers have often established unequal, top-down relationships with families, in which teachers were the experts and families were supposed to be passive recipients of this expertise. However, current thinking about family–school relationships has come a long way from that traditional model. In its position statement on developmentally appropriate practice, NAEYC (2008) recommends that teacher–family relationships should be "reciprocal"—in other words, the relationship should be characterized by mutual respect and exchange of ideas. NAEYC's early childhood program standards expect high-quality programs to establish and maintain "collaborative relationships with each child's family to foster development in all settings. These relationships are sensitive to family composition, language, and culture" (NAEYC, 2005a, p. 11).

What Can Early Childhood Educators Do to Strengthen Relationships with Families?

First, it is important to keep in mind that most families want to have close relationships with their young child's program and staff. Although they may encounter logistical barriers, single parents and young families have been found to be especially eager for relationships with their child's teacher and early childhood program, especially when it comes to children's social and emotional development (Olson & Hyson, 2005).

Many resources are available to help early childhood professionals build caring relationships characterized by respect, care, appreciation of family strengths, and mutual enjoyment (see NAEYC, 2006; Weiss et al., 2006). Janis Keyser's book *From Parents to Partners* (2006) is an especially rich source of practical suggestions.

Relationships are built on personal knowledge and interaction, so a good starting point is to quickly learn the names of each important person in the child's family (stepparents, siblings, grandparents, etc.). If family members bring their children to the program, staff can make sure that every family and child is greeted upon arrival. Teachers can also learn about some significant interest or characteristic of each family member. Of course, the most important interest that families and teachers have in common is the child. Families warm up quickly to staff who show they enjoy and know their child. It can be difficult to find time to have even brief discussions with families, but staff coverage can be arranged so that teachers can chat with family members at arrival and drop-off without leaving children unsupervised.

These and other steps usually create the basis for positive relationships, but not always. Sometimes relationship-building difficulties arise because of differences between the teacher's cultural traditions and those of the family. For example, the staff in the program highlighted in the opening vignette have found that many Central American families are reluctant to share personal information with outsiders. Furthermore, in this and many other cultures, teachers are regarded as authority figures and experts. Families within these cultural traditions may feel uncomfortable when teachers try to establish a more informal, equal relationship. Again, resources can help early childhood educators to better understand diverse cultural traditions, as well as differences *within* cultures, and to use this understanding to create caring, respectful, and culturally responsive relationships (Lynch & Hanson, 2004; Quintero, 1999).

At other times, relationships may be difficult to establish because family members have had negative experiences with schools or teachers, either in their own growing-up or when their children were enrolled in other programs. Because of these experiences, they may feel defensive, inadequate, or anxious about having any kind of relationship with their child's teacher. By creating informal opportunities for families to get to know staff as well as other families (a family lounge or corner with comfortable seating, a pizza night, work parties), those families with negative prior experiences may begin to feel that they now belong to a supportive community in which they are known and respected. These issues led the highlighted program's prekindergarten teachers and family advisors to use part of their budget to offer coffee and pastries every Friday morning, inviting informal morning get-togethers in an alcove near the classrooms.

TOOL 2: APPROACHES-TO-LEARNING CONVERSATIONS WITH FAMILIES

With the foundation for a respectful, reciprocal relationship established, teachers can more easily involve families in conversations that focus on children's approaches to learning.

Why, When, and Where?

Talking with and listening to families, teachers gain insight into children's interests and learning behaviors at home, and into their families' beliefs about how best to motivate and engage their children. With the kind of assessment information suggested in Chapter 8, teachers can also help families notice and appreciate the signs of children's growing curiosity, planning skills, and other signs of enthusiasm and engagement. These conversations may also reveal that some families may not be promoting positive approaches to learning or achievement goals because they see few opportunities for their children to succeed when they grow up (Ogbu, 1985).

Conversations that focus on children's approaches to learning can take place almost anytime and anywhere. Whether they happen briefly as family members are dropping off or picking up their children, in scheduled parent conferences, as part of regular meetings with families of all the children in a class during family meetings, or in other formats, these conversations help families and practitioners learn from one another.

Getting Conversations Started

It is not always easy to get a good conversation going, no matter who is the conversational partner. The general suggestions below are adapted from Keyser (2006); I added examples to specifically focus on the topic of children's approaches to learning.

- Show sincere interest in the family and the child, asking family members open-ended questions (e.g., *"I would love to know more about where Angelo gets his wonderful excitement about drawing. Is this something that your family does at home?"*).
- Share something about yourself (e.g., *"You know, when I was Angelo's age, I was always drawing pictures, too. When I got older, I took some art classes, and I still love to draw."*).
- Notice and respond to families' individual or culturally influenced communication styles (e.g., *If you sense that Angelo's grandmother doesn't seem comfortable chatting casually about her grandson on the playground, you might say, "Maybe you would like to come into the office later, so we can*

talk about how to help Angelo apply his interest in drawing to other parts of his school work. I would really love to hear your ideas about that.").

Conversation Topics: Components of Enthusiasm and Engagement

All components of approaches to learning are potentially useful topics for conversations with one family member, an extended family, or a group of families. For example, most parents love to talk about their children's interests and about what gives them special pleasure. As parent and teacher watch a toddler at the sandbox in the afternoon, the teacher can comment about the child's motivation and persistence, helping the parent to see how persistently the child is trying to use the shovel and how she keeps at it even when the sand spills out. Similarly, if a parent is looking at a book with her child before leaving for work, a teacher might comment that she's noticed that the child's attention is so much more focused when the parent sits close to her and points out the pictures on each page. When another child cries but is able to calm himself after being upset when his father leaves, the teacher might point out to the father that this self-regulation is a step forward for his son. Teachers can help families understand that each of these examples reflects a positive approach to learning, which will contribute to their child's emotional, social, and academic development.

Some approaches-to-learning conversations will naturally bring up cultural preferences and expectations. For example, there may be opportunities to talk about why it is important for children to ask their teacher questions, even though such questioning may not be part of some cultural traditions. If positive relationships exist, families and early childhood staff can understand and explore these issues together.

When Conversations Can Be Difficult

Just as relationship-building can be difficult, some conversations about children's approaches to learning can challenge teachers and families. Once parents understand how important their children's approaches to learning are, some may put undue pressure on their children to be more focused or persistent. This is a time when some child development information may help, if it is presented in a low-key way. For example, parents need to know that it's normal for toddlers to shift their attention quickly from one activity to another, or to be easily frustrated. It is reassuring for families to understand these age-related limitations while also looking for and supporting signs of progress.

Sometimes more significant approaches-to-learning problems arise. The problem may be one that the family has identified, or it may be one that the teacher has observed but that the family has not yet seen as a difficulty. In either case, it is important to structure a conversation about the problem so that it is a true, respectful dialogue with outcomes that are satisfactory both to the family and to the early childhood professional. Figure 9.2 includes suggestions and examples that may be adapted to a variety of approaches-to-learning issues.

⩕ **FIGURE 9.2   Nuts and Bolts: Tips for Talking with Families About Problems Related to Approaches to Learning**

Keyser (2006, pp. 48–50) lists these suggestions for having productive conversations during problem-solving meetings with parents. Such conversations might occur during regularly scheduled conferences or during a specially arranged meeting. I have followed each tip with an example from a hypothetical discussion in which a kindergarten teacher is meeting with 6-year-old Carol's single father to discuss aspects of her approaches to learning.

◆ Listen, listen, listen. Ask open-ended questions, and reflect back to the parent. (*"It sounds like you have been worried that Carol is unmotivated when it comes to learning to read. What are you seeing at home that makes you worry about that?"*)

◆ Restate and reframe the parent's ideas. (*Carol's father has just said his daughter is a "lazy scatterbrain." Teacher: "So, you're seeing that Carol gets pretty distracted and forgetful sometimes, and she seems not to be trying very hard."*)

◆ Acknowledge the parent's efforts and strengths. (*"It must be really hard to deal with Carol's frustration, when it's the end of a long day, you're trying to help her with her reading, and she wants to give up. It's amazing how you've been handling the new job and moving to a new city all at the same time."*)

◆ Ask the parent what he or she would like to happen. (*"When you think about Carol's motivation to read, what changes would you like to see?"*)

◆ Give child development information as appropriate. (*"You know, children Carol's age are starting to notice how they do in comparison to other children, and because of this, sometimes they get discouraged or avoid things where they might fail. Usually that changes when they start to figure out how to help themselves learn, and when they experience even a little success."*)

◆ Refer the parent to resources. (*"You might want to talk with Julia's parents—I remember that she was having similar difficulties a while back. And this brochure—*Raising a Reader, Raising a Writer*—has some tips for things to do at home that might really spark Carol's interest again."*)

◆ Make a plan to check back with the parent, and thank the parent for sharing with you. (*"Thank you so much for sharing your experiences and concerns. I think I can come up with some new ideas now about how to help Carol become more motivated to learn to read, and I hope you feel better about this, also. Let's keep in touch and check in on how things are going in a few weeks."*)

TOOL 3: PRACTICAL IDEAS TO SHARE WITH FAMILIES

This tool has been saved for last, because no matter how good the practical ideas may be, families will not be receptive to "parent education" or other interventions unless there is a positive relationship (Kelly & Barnard, 1999) and unless teachers have already engaged families in a variety of supportive, culturally responsive conversations.

Assuming the program has helped families gain an understanding of what positive approaches to learning are, and why they are important, families may have more specific questions. These may include

- What are the most important things that our family can do to help our child become more enthusiastic about and engaged in learning?
- What home activities will be the best ones to increase our child's positive approaches to learning?
- Would it be good for us to get involved in our child's activities and, if so, how?

Reassurance and Reminders for Families

Without being prescriptive, teachers can indeed share ideas in response to these kinds of questions, whether the questions are asked directly or are read between the lines. Parents may appreciate being reminded that a warm, secure, encouraging relationship with their child is the most valuable gift they can give. Parents may also need assurance that external rewards are not required to motivate their children to learn, and in fact that these rewards can backfire, undermining motivation. Instead, ideas can be shared about how parents can emphasize "learning goals" and children's effort, rather than simply focusing on successful performance. A parent meeting could be a good time to think about and perhaps role play the language that helps get this message across to children (e.g., "I see how hard you are working on that birthday card for your sister. You have stuck with it for a long time!").

Early childhood educators can introduce other suggestions for families to consider. For example, parents, grandparents, and other family members can let their children see them showing interest in all sorts of things, from car repair to baking to politics. Family members can also demonstrate how to stick with a difficult task, talking out loud about what they are doing and why ("This paint is still not mixed enough—see the streaks? My arm's getting tired, but I guess I had better stir it some more so that it will look nice on our walls"). Parents can also notice and support their child's interests: For example, they can create opportunities for a child who is interested in math to use his developing knowledge to help his parents with shopping, sorting household materials, and other important tasks.

Parents may also appreciate reminders that young children need plenty of time to explore their ideas and work on projects, whether these are joint projects with adults or things they do on their own. Parents can extend children's attention and persistence by finding ways for children to continue an art project or keep reading a new book over several days.

When families wonder how much they should get involved in their children's learning, they may value some reminders that a balance is important. Young children do need adults' support and security if they are to develop positive approaches to learning, but at times adults need to withdraw this support so children can tackle learning tasks independently. The example of children doing puzzles is one that many adults understand—most adults spontaneously give the child hints or move a piece almost into place. This is a form of adult scaffolding: helping children stay engaged and be successful without completely taking over. In making these suggestions, though, early childhood educators will need to be sensitive to wide cultural variations in how parents help their children develop skills—ranging from direct instruction to demonstration to scaffolded guidance (Rogoff, 2003).

Depending on families' needs, interests, and circumstances, many other ideas may be drawn from chapters in this book, especially Chapter 6 on curriculum and Chapter 7 on teaching practices. Although the ideas in those chapters are aimed at teachers, their essential features can easily be adapted for family members. Deborah Stipek and Kathy Seal's book *Motivated Minds: Raising Children to Love Learning* (2001) is written for parents and is filled with down-to-earth ideas that parents can use with children of different ages. Another book, by Judy Helm and colleagues, suggests ways that families can build on young children's interests to do challenging, engaging project work at home (Helm, Berg, & Scranton, 2004).

Where and How to Share Practical Ideas

Sharing these kinds of approaches-to-learning ideas can happen in a number of settings. These include informal chats with one or a few parents and other family members, newsletters or other print and electronic communication (Diffily & Morrison, 1996), bulletin boards in a parent area, or classroom- or school-wide parent meetings. Parent meetings are most effective if families get to participate actively, perhaps experimenting in small groups with the kinds of activities their children are doing, or trying out adult-level puzzles or brain teasers to get a sense of how it feels to be challenged by something new and possibly confusing (Keyser, 2006). Parents can also view documentation of their children's work (posted examples, slides, video, etc.), talking together about what it shows in terms of children's interest in learning, persistence and engagement. As the prekindergarten team in the opening vignette planned their series of family meetings, they included many of these ideas.

Home visits offer other opportunities. Figure 9.3 invites you to think about how home visits, an optional or required part of many early childhood programs, could be enhanced to partner with families about approaches to learning.

❧ FIGURE 9.3   Enhancing the Everyday: Home Visiting and Approaches to Learning

In many early childhood programs, teaching staff make visits to each child's home; Head Start requires a minimum of two such visits each year. A primary purpose of home visits is to keep parents informed about their child's growth and development. Other purposes often include better meeting the needs of children and their families, setting the stage for joint problem-solving, learning more about children by seeing them at home, and encouraging parents to become involved. Some home visiting programs include direct teaching of the child; additionally, teachers may be able to give families who are under stress some additional support and resources (Michigan Department of Education Early Childhood Programs, 1999). Often, home visits include both discussion with family members and some kind of activity involving the child and family, or perhaps demonstrated by the teacher/home visitor.

Within the basic framework of home visiting, how could the typical beginning-of-year visit be enriched to have more emphasis on children's approaches to learning? Think about ways to discuss a child's enthusiasm and engagement during such a visit, to explore a family's beliefs and values, and to plan specific activities that will help parents and other family members both understand their child's enthusiasm and engagement and gain more ideas about how to promote these attitudes and behaviors.

Supporting Families = Supporting Their Children's Positive Approaches to Learning

Although some families might want to be given a recipe that yields highly motivated, fully engaged, interested young learners, no such recipe exists. As we have seen in this chapter, although families may welcome specific information and tips about promoting positive approaches to learning, it is the broader context of family support that is most important. Early childhood programs that give families this kind of support will help create environments in which enthusiasm and engagement can flourish. Families who are themselves respected, listened to, and supported are better able to give their children supportive relationships and experiences.

This requires what increasingly is described as "family-centered care" or "family-centered services" (Keyser, 2006; Pletcher & McBride, 2004; Sandall, McLean, & Smith, 2000). As summarized by Keyser, and consistent with principles articulated in health services, child welfare, early intervention, and early childhood special education, the key principles of family-centered care include

- Recognizing and respecting one another's knowledge and expertise
- Sharing information through two-way communication
- Sharing power and decision-making
- Acknowledging and respecting diversity
- Creating networks of support (Keyser, p. 12).

This chapter has emphasized these principles specifically in terms of work-ing with families to promote young children's positive approaches to learn-ing—but the principles need to be consistently implemented in all aspects of family relationships.

LOOKING BACK AND LOOKING FORWARD

The theme of Part II of this book has been "Transforming Risks into Opportuni-ties." So far I have described five sets of evidence-based tools that can be used to create these opportunities. Although they have been presented in separate chapters, to be most effective these tools need to be used together. For example, without close family involvement and collaboration with staff, curriculum (Chapter 6), teaching practices (Chapter 7), and assessment (Chapter 8) will be less influential in supporting enthusiasm and engagement. And families will be more likely to become involved in reciprocal relationships with staff (Chapter 9) if they see teachers genuinely enjoying and building secure relationships with their children (Chapter 5).

These tools are all intended to be used within individual classrooms and programs, by teachers and other staff who are convinced of the importance of children's approaches to learning. But how do we get from this conviction to wider advocacy and action? The final chapter will take up this challenge.

Reflection, Discussion, and Action

1. Interview one or two families to gain insight into their beliefs about children's approaches to learning. If you are working with colleagues, discuss possible topics and questions in advance, keeping in mind cultural responsiveness and avoiding "educationese" jargon. Consider how these insights could help you as an early childhood educator.

2. Identify a child who seems to be having difficulty in one or more of the components of positive approaches to learning. For example, perhaps this child is very distractible, or has difficulty persisting at a challenging task, or appears uninterested in classroom activities. Plan how you might have a conversation with family members about these issues, using suggestions in this chapter and other resources. What outcomes would you hope to achieve, and how would you engage the family in an authentic partnership to support the child's development?

3. Use the principles and recommendations in this chapter to plan one or more family meetings around some aspect of approaches to learning. If possible, implement and evaluate the plans, or seek feedback on the plans from your colleagues.

10

Tools to Create Change

Thirty people are seated around a conference table. They have been appointed by the recently elected governor of their state to develop a vision for the state's early care and education system. Chaired by a senior member of the Governor's Office for Children, the group includes representation from the child care, family child care, prekindergarten, and Head Start communities; higher education; relevant state and nonprofit agencies; and families.

Several of those in the room are concerned that the state's emphasis on early literacy has come at the expense of young children's social and emotional development, critical thinking, and positive approaches to learning. At the opening meeting, the chairperson brings up this issue and asks the task force to spend time reaching consensus about whether changes are needed in the state's priorities and, if so, what actions would be needed to create change—on which fronts and with what tools.

AS SUGGESTED by the opening vignette, this chapter takes us beyond classrooms and family contexts to consider other ways in which the early childhood profession can influence young children's approaches to learning. First, in Figure 10.1 I will revisit research that documents the risk that children will become discouraged and disengaged learners. Then I will suggest five tools that may help create systemic, sustainable change: first, a *theory of change and a logic model to get there*; second, *relevant, persuasive research*; third, *professional development* for current and future early childhood educators; and fourth, *effective advocacy* to create more emphasis on approaches to learning. Finally, *knowledge utilization strategies* can increase the probability that approaches-to-learning knowledge will be incorporated into policies, practices, and professional development systems.

❖ FIGURE 10.1   Research Reminders: Risks to Enthusiasm and Engagement

- Teachers from prekindergarten through third grade frequently use lengthy whole-group instruction with an emphasis on rote learning. These kinds of teaching strategies are associated with lower levels of interest and involvement (NICHD Early Child Care Research Network, 2005).
- Close teacher–child relationships predict greater persistence and enthusiasm for learning, yet children observed in the National Prekindergarten Study were directly involved with teachers and other adults less than one third of the time (Clifford et al., 2005; Pianta et al., 2005).
- At home and in school, external rewards for achievement appear to decrease students' engagement and achievement motivation (Gottfried et al., 1994, 1998; National Research Council, 2003).
- Increasingly, state standards influence what gets taught and what gets assessed, yet fewer than half of the states have explicitly included approaches to learning in their early learning standards (Scott-Little et al., 2005).
- High-stakes accountability pressures have been especially detrimental to the motivation of children who begin school with low achievement or who are disaffected by school, even in the early grades (Kumar et al., 2002).
- Ethnic minority children, especially boys, are likely to develop problems with motivation to learn, often because the curriculum and teaching practices do not connect with their interests or styles of interaction (Barbarin, 2002; Graham & Taylor, 2002).

Goals of This Chapter

After reading this chapter, you will be better able to

1. Assess the need to create changes in the early childhood system, so that all children may develop more positive approaches to learning.
2. Work with others to identify desired outcomes and plan steps to reach those outcomes.
3. Draw upon a variety of resources to create sustainable change.

TOOL 1: A THEORY OF CHANGE AND A LOGIC MODEL TO GET THERE

The state task force will have greater impact if the group begins by identifying the results it wants for young children. For example, perhaps the members agree that the most pressing need is for children to be more eager to learn, motivated primarily by their own curiosity and desire to master challenging content.

What actions will be likely to influence that outcome for the state's young children? Answering that question will help clarify the group's "theory of change"—the assumptions and evidence base that can guide their decisions about needed actions (Anderson, 2004; Organizational Research Services, 2004). Perhaps the task force looks at evidence from research, and from the experiences of professionals and families. This investigation might persuade the task force that (1) family–child and teacher–child relationships are a key to bringing about this outcome and (2) certain kinds of early childhood curriculum and teaching practices are also likely to bring about the desired motivational results.

The task force also believes that certain education policies currently in force in their state—for example, a school readiness test that focuses on a small number of literacy and mathematical skills—are likely to undermine the results they are trying to achieve. And they think that the new governor may be open to looking at children's motivation and engagement in learning as important school readiness outcomes. Finally, in a recent statewide survey, many families of primary-grade children reported that their children's interest in school is decreasing rather than increasing.

Guided by this kind of analysis, one can begin to map out a pathway or "logic model" (Harris, 2001) that links desired outcomes (both ultimate goals and shorter term impacts) to specific activities or strategies likely to bring about the results. For example, the task force thinks a policy summit might be a good way to bring together state legislators and others who are in a position to create approaches-to-learning policy changes. Also, the state early childhood education organization may decide to make approaches to learning the theme of its annual professional development conference. These are just a few examples; whatever

---

❧ **FIGURE 10.2   Nuts and Bolts: Web-Based Resources to Use in Developing Theories of Change and Logic Models**

- ◆ *Theory of Change.* A Web site developed by ActKnowledge and The Aspen Institute Roundtable on Community Change. Includes definitions, online tools and resources, links to printed reports, and more. http://www.theoryofchange.org/index.html
- ◆ *Planning and Evaluation Resource Center.* Links to many tools and resources to develop theories of change and logic models, with community examples. http://www.evaluationtools.org/plan_theory.asp
- ◆ *Evaluation: Start Here Please! The Community Health Worker Evaluation Tool Kit.* Developed at the University of Arizona with support from the Annie E. Casey Foundation, this tool kit includes a very practical "Logic Model Development Guide." http://www.publichealth.arizona.edu/chwtoolkit/PDFs/Logicmod/logicmod.pdf

---

the specifics may be, the purpose of such a logic model is to align and coordinate activities to bring about a set of well-defined outcomes, avoiding a flurry of nice-sounding but uncoordinated and ineffective actions. Figure 10.2 lists a few "Nuts and Bolts" resources for those who want to develop theory-of-change logic models. The Action Planning Form in Appendix B may also help guide your thinking.

TOOL 2: RELEVANT, PERSUASIVE RESEARCH

The state task force will have difficulty developing its logic model without research to identify those actions that are most likely to influence children's approaches to learning. As we have seen, there is a good deal of research from which to draw, but the research base remains inadequate in several respects.

Research Needs

This book has summarized research about various dimensions and components of approaches to learning. This sort of information is potentially useful to those trying to create change. However, the research may be difficult to find and synthesize, since it has been done under so many different labels, not just "approaches to learning." Additionally, the research not been readily accessible to early childhood educators, advocates, teacher educators, and other practitioners. A high-level, systematic review and integration of this body of work, similar to the National Research Council's syntheses of research on other topics, would be of great benefit to the early childhood field.

Although there is considerable research on specific topics related to approaches to learning, there are also major gaps in what we know. For example, I have already noted that most of the approaches-to-learning research has been conducted with White, middle-class children and families. Studies in this area should reflect all forms of diversity and should examine variations within as well as among ethnic and racial groups. The approaches-to-learning research also has gaps in the age groups that have been studied. For example, interesting work has been done on motivation and school engagement, but much of it includes elementary and secondary school students rather than younger children.

Those who are planning and implementing early childhood programs would certainly like to see more research about how to validly assess children's enthusiasm and engagement (see also Chapter 8). Very little is now available to help classroom teachers or program directors understand children's approaches to learning or evaluate a program's effectiveness in this area.

Finally, little research has been conducted about approaches-to-learning interventions. Although we can use more general curriculum and teaching research to make some inferences about the curriculum approaches and classroom practices that may be effective in promoting enthusiasm and engagement, well-validated classroom interventions such as those that have been developed in other areas such as literacy, mathematics, or social skills are only beginning to emerge.

Setting Research Priorities

To create change, researchers and others must influence priorities to support major research syntheses and to fund new, well-designed studies whose results will be useful to decision makers such as the members of the state task force in the opening vignette. To be most effective, this effort needs the voices and collaboration of practitioners as well as policy makers; both groups know first-hand the dilemmas of implementation and can identify questions to which they need answers. For example, in the state task force are leaders of several nonprofit agencies serving immigrant and refugee families. Leaders of these agencies must decide on their priorities for early childhood services, yet they find little evidence-based guidance on how to promote positive approaches to learning for these culturally diverse immigrant children, many of whom have been traumatized by conflict and famine. The voices of these leaders need to be heard in discussions about future research priorities.

Promising Directions in Research

Despite the wide range of research needs, new directions in applied research show promise for the future. For example, the work of John Fantuzzo and colleagues is leading to development of a new, evidence-based curriculum for preschool teachers to use in targeting specific learning behaviors, including frustration tolerance, attention control, group learning, and task approach (Fantuzzo et al., 2008; Rouse & Fantuzzo, 2008). Robin McWilliam's program of research on engagement, beginning with but not restricted to children with disabilities, is leading to concrete, evidence-based recommendations about assessing and supporting engagement in classrooms (McWilliam & Casey, 2007). Also in the area of assessment, work by McClelland and colleagues (2007) may help teachers learn more about how children's self-regulation and use of executive function develop, and how these may influence later outcomes in early reading, vocabulary, and math. Research on various components of approaches to learning is on the verge of filling many gaps in our knowledge base: This is good news for those like the members of the state task force, as well as advocates, policy makers, teachers, and professional development specialists.

TOOL 3: NEW APPROACHES TO PROFESSIONAL DEVELOPMENT

Professional development in early childhood education has become a topic of keen interest (Zaslow & Martinez-Beck, 2005). It is clear that high-quality early childhood teachers make a difference for children. It is less clear whether degrees themselves, the specific *type* of professional development, or some combination of both, are the critical factors in bringing about positive child outcomes (Early et al., 2007; Winton, McCollum, & Catlett, 2007). In this section I will examine what is needed so that professional development can be a tool for change in young children's approaches to learning—focusing on both content and process, and looking at preservice and inservice education.

Content

In general, approaches to learning are not strongly represented as a content emphasis at either the inservice or preservice level. Despite increasing awareness that children's approaches to learning are important and that they can be positively influenced by their teachers, too little professional development has focused on this aspect of development and learning. To be sure, professional development often includes an emphasis on social and emotional development, but even in that domain teachers may not learn enough about how to intentionally promote positive development (Shonkoff & Phillips, 2000). Similarly, when professional development addresses cognitive and academic domains, the emphasis is usually on what children should learn, and how to help them learn this content, rather than on how teachers can nurture children's enthusiasm and engagement in learning.

Processes

In the work of the state task force and in other cases, it would certainly be valuable to emphasize approaches to learning as a professional development content area. However, the *processes* used in that professional development need at least as much attention as the content. Early childhood professional development, and teacher education in general, have been criticized for relying on isolated, one-shot workshops that do not reflect current research on how people learn and that have little effect on practice (Bransford, Brown, & Cocking, 1999; Winton et al., 2007). In its first meeting, for example, the state task force learns that the state NAEYC organization intends to use "Approaches to Learning" as its professional development conference theme. This is an exciting possibility, but the conference content alone will not create changes in teachers' practice. If the task force can encourage the organization to include practitioners in planning the conference, and if some kind of follow-up mentoring, coaching, or consultation can be added (perhaps with additional support from the Governor's office), it is much more likely that early childhood programs will actually change their practices and sustain those changes over time.

The preceding observations and suggestions apply to both preservice and inservice professional development. However, because there are also some distinctive issues in each, we will now look at preservice and inservice issues separately.

Preservice issues. To a great extent, the content and processes of preservice teacher education are driven by national and state standards for what future early childhood educators should know and be able to do. NAEYC's standards for early childhood professional preparation have been influential, especially through their use in NAEYC's national recognition of higher education programs and accreditation by the National Council for Accreditation of Teacher Education (NCATE) (Hyson, 2003; Hyson & Biggar, 2005). However, the standards themselves do not mention approaches to learning specifically, although the narrative discussion of Standard 1 (Child Development and Learning) says that "young children's characteristics and needs" include their "learning processes and motivation to learn" (Hyson, 2003, p. 30). It would be desirable for future revisions of the standards to further highlight this area of teacher competence, emphasizing the need for appropriate learning opportunities for future teachers and for assessment of teacher candidates' ability to support children's enthusiasm and engagement.

Besides attention to the standards for early childhood professional preparation, faculty development is needed to strengthen preservice education. A recent Web survey of faculty in associate's and baccalaureate early childhood programs showed that many faculty lack knowledge of current theory and research and have little support for their own professional development (Hyson, Tomlinson, & Lutton, 2007). Although the survey did not specifically ask about approaches to learning, the faculty knowledge gap probably includes this body of recent research as well as others.

In addition to benefiting from their professors' knowledge about approaches to learning, preservice students will also need enhanced hands-on experiences, observing children's approaches to learning and developing and evaluating the effects of different curricula and teaching methods on children's enthusiasm and engagement. When preservice programs assess their students' effects on children's learning (an NCATE accreditation requirement), those assessments should include student teachers' effects on children's interest, engagement, attention, persistence, self-regulation, and other approaches-to-learning components.

Inservice issues. Just as preservice programs are driven by national and state standards, so inservice professional development is increasingly influenced by what is emphasized in states' early learning standards and what is emphasized in states' teacher competencies and their early childhood professional development plans (Scott-Little, Lesko, Martella, & Milburn, 2007). Nebraska is an example of a state that has explicit emphasis on approaches to learning in its standards and is now creating inservice professional development to help teachers promote these outcomes. In contrast, those states that have little emphasis on approaches-to-learning outcomes are unlikely to have much emphasis on this domain in their professional development plans. However, there are opportunities to embed this content in any state's professional development system, and bodies such as state task forces may be in a good position to recommend such actions.

Staff diversity is also important to consider when planning inservice professional development on approaches-to-learning issues. Typical in community-based training, this diversity includes a wide range of education and experience as well as cultural and linguistic diversity. Teachers from diverse cultures can be expected to have diverse ideas about what children's positive approaches to learning look like. They are also likely to hold diverse opinions about how adults should support children in developing enthusiasm and engagement. Effective inservice education has to respect these differences, engaging program staff in reflective, facilitated dialogue and drawing from the wisdom of practice.

TOOL 4: EFFECTIVE ADVOCACY

As described in Chapter 4 and summarized in Figure 10.1, many risks to children's positive approaches to learning have stemmed from public policies that overlook or even undermine enthusiasm and engagement. To reduce these risks and create new opportunities, effective advocacy is needed (Robinson & Stark, 2005).

What is advocacy? Some people assume that all advocacy occurs at the federal policy level, influencing Congress or the White House to do things differently. Sometimes that is the case, but advocacy at other levels can be equally effective. There can be advocacy at the personal level: for example, when a member of the early childhood task force sits down for coffee with a few fellow program directors and begins a discussion of what has happened to children's joy in learning, and what the directors might do about this, together. Private-sector advocacy is also useful, as when the task force decides that there is not enough involvement of the business community and asks members of the Chamber of Commerce or the business roundtable whether task force members might come to one of their meetings to get their reactions to the task force's plans.

Within the domain of approaches to learning, what might be some targets and issues for advocacy? Obviously these will vary at different times and places. A few issues that may offer windows of opportunity are the following:

- The presence or absence of approaches to learning in the state's early learning standards
- The place of approaches to learning in the state's early childhood professional development plans and in its higher education system
- The ways in which children are being assessed in local education programs—is there attention to approaches to learning and are appropriate assessment methods being used?
- Whether approaches-to-learning effects are being considered in decisions about early childhood curriculum and recommended teaching practices.

Such issues can be addressed through all kinds of advocacy—personal, private-sector, and public policy advocacy—and at either the local, state, or national level. A logic model, developed with the methods outlined earlier in this chapter, will be very helpful in focusing on desired outcomes and identifying actions—in this case, advocacy—to create those outcomes.

Whatever the type of advocacy, it will be essential to have a few core messages that are used clearly and consistently. It is worth taking the time to craft these messages well, perhaps testing the language with focus groups and different kinds of audiences. Figure 10.3 gives an example of a few core messages about approaches to learning.

Advocates are just beginning to appreciate what a difference it makes to frame issues in certain ways. The FrameWorks Institute has pioneered in helping organizations think about how their key issues are framed and how the public reacts when the issues are framed in different ways. For example, FrameWorks researchers

---

❧ FIGURE 10.3   Nuts and Bolts: Key Messages About Approaches to Learning

- Approaches to learning are behaviors and attitudes that show *how* children learn, not just *what* they learn.
- Approaches to learning include children's enthusiasm for learning (such as their interest, pleasure, and motivation to learn) and their engagement in learning (such as their attention, persistence, flexibility, and self-regulation).
- Children begin to develop these characteristics and behaviors at an early age, and even in the early years children show enormous differences in these dimensions.
- These differences can influence children's school readiness and school success.
- Children's experiences at home and in early childhood programs can strengthen or undermine their positive approaches to learning.
- Early childhood programs can promote positive approaches to learning through relationships, curriculum, program environments and teaching practices, appropriate assessments, and family involvement.
- Sustainable, system-wide changes in policies and practices are necessary to build positive approaches to learning.

found that despite much publicity and advocacy, many in the public still do not understand what the science of child development is showing about school readiness and why school readiness matters (Aubrun & Grady, 2002). By intentionally creating clear, simple messages and other tools that reframe the issues, advocates and others make it more likely that the public will become engaged in creating positive change. Consistent with these recommendations, simple messages about why it is important for children to be interested and motivated to learn may connect effectively with parents and other stakeholders.

TOOL 5: STRATEGIES TO IMPLEMENT KNOWLEDGE ABOUT APPROACHES TO LEARNING

As summarized by Buysse and Wesley (2005), "evidence-based practice" integrates the best available research with the expertise, wisdom, and values of families and practitioners. This is as true in the area of approaches to learning as it is elsewhere. However, scholars in developmental and educational research increasingly realize that this evidence base alone is not enough to create changes in policies and practices (Huston, 2005; Shonkoff, 2000). The relatively new field of implementation research shows that the most well-documented interventions—whether in public health, mental health, education, or other fields—will not be effectively implemented merely because the research shows that they "work" (Fixsen, Naoom, Blase, Friedman, & Wallace, 2005). If the state task force tries this strategy (just publishing guidelines for good approaches-to-learning policies and practices, for example), they will be disappointed with the results.

What is the solution? No easy remedies exist, but a growing body of work with names such as knowledge utilization, knowledge transfer, knowledge exchange, and implementation research offers some direction. For example, several writers (Bogenschneider & Gross, 2004; Cohn, 2006) have pointed out that policy makers are looking not so much for isolated research findings as for broad "schools of thought" on a particular issue. Knowledge about why enthusiasm and engagement are important, and how to strengthen these attitudes and behaviors, may be such a school of thought, helping policy makers make sense of some of the complex problems they face. Used in this way, research can create a general awareness that something is not going well in children's lives and can suggest some general directions for improvement.

A potentially effective way to bring such knowledge to bear on policy, discussed by McCabe (2007), is to create something like the "Family Impact Seminars" (Bogenschneider, Olson, Linney, & Mills, 2000) that have linked legislative staff and other policy makers to relevant family research. The planning for these seminars and follow-up reports incorporates feedback about their specific needs. Various aspects of approaches to learning (or, in more down-to-earth language, children's enthusiasm and engagement) may be an attractive option for this kind of regular meeting among researchers, policy makers, and practitioners.

LOOKING BACK AND LOOKING FORWARD: CONCLUDING THOUGHTS

In *Enthusiastic and Engaged Learners: Approaches to Learning in the Early Childhood Classroom*, I have tried to convey both the critical importance of young children's approaches to learning and the many practical strategies available to strengthen their enthusiasm and engagement. In terms of the circles of influence that were introduced in Chapter 3, I have moved from considering individual children's characteristics; to programs' curricula, teaching practices, and assessment methods; to families; and finally to the wider context of creating systemic change. Now I would like to take a final look back at the children themselves.

Throughout this book, I have emphasized that our approaches-to-learning efforts must meet the needs of all children, whatever their cultures, circumstances, abilities, and disabilities. It is especially important to remember that the children who most need positive approaches to learning are often those who are most at risk of becoming discouraged and disengaged. If this negative pattern starts in the early years, it is likely to lead into a cycle of less interest, lower motivation to learn, diminished ability to persist and self-regulate, and—as a result—increased risk of academic failure.

But with our help, *all* children can become enthusiastic about and engaged in learning. I hope this book will strengthen our collective commitment to bring about that result, so that children's approaches to learning will bring them happiness today and will lead to more effective learning in the future.

 Reflection, Discussion, and Action

1. With some colleagues, try using the Theory-of-Change/Logic Model framework to make plans for changes in children's approaches to learning. You might identify some specific short-term and longer term outcomes and map out activities that are likely to produce those outcomes.

2. Again with others, try engaging in some advocacy about approaches to learning. This might be personal advocacy, policy advocacy (at the local, state, or national level), or advocacy with the business community or other private-sector groups. Use the resources suggested in this chapter to sharpen your advocacy skills.

3. If message development is important to your work, you might take the Key Messages in Figure 10.3 and adapt these to different audiences or potential stakeholders.

4. What are some opportunities to embed a greater emphasis on approaches to learning in preservice or inservice professional development? Depending on your own situation, you might select one area for special focus. What content might be embedded, and with what processes of professional development? What resources would be needed by teacher educators or inservice professional development specialists?

APPENDIX A

Examples of Developmental Changes in Children's Approaches to Learning

RESEARCH SHOWS that if children start school with a strong set of attitudes and skills that help them "learn how to learn," they will be better able to take advantage of educational opportunities. While some learning skills come naturally to children, others can be developed through a supportive environment.

Adapted from "Child development tracker: Approaches to learning," *PBS Parents guide to child development*. Retrieved March 5, 2008, from http://www.pbs.org/parents/childdevelopment/. Reprinted from pbsparents.org with permission of the Public Broadcasting Service.

	1–2 years	2–3 years	3–4 years	4–5 years	5–6 years
Snapshots	One-year-olds are in the act of discovering the world. They enthusiastically use their senses to purposefully explore everything they can. They find pleasure in causing things to happen and in completing basic tasks. They also enjoy sharing interesting learning experiences with adults, and may use gestures and simple sounds or speech to ask adults questions. Since language skills are still developing, one-year-olds rely more heavily on nonverbal, physical strategies to reach simple goals.	Two-year-olds enjoy using their senses to explore the world, and can solve simple problems with the "trial and error" method. They will practice an activity many times to master it, and can complete short-term, concrete tasks. Their budding language skills and desire to learn prompt many "why," "what," and "how" questions. This year typically marks the beginning of pretend play, where two-year-olds experiment with familiar objects and situations to process their experiences.	Three-year-olds increasingly know what they want and express their preferences. While playing, they are better able to ignore distractions and focus on the task at hand. They will even persist in completing something that is a bit difficult. Learning still happens primarily through exploring, using all the senses. Their growing language skills allow for more complex questions and discussion, and they can think more creatively and methodically when solving problems.	When it comes to learning, four-year-olds are developing greater self-control and ingenuity. Their pretend play is more complex and imaginative, and can be sustained for longer periods. They can also make plans and complete tasks. Four-year-olds want to try new experiences. They also want to be more self-reliant, and seek to expand the areas of their lives where they can be independent decision-makers.	Five-year-olds are creative and enthusiastic problem solvers. They offer progressively more imaginative ideas for how to do a task, make something, or solve longer-term or more abstract challenges. As they participate in a variety of new experiences, five-year-olds ask more analytical questions and weigh their choices. They are also more social as they learn new things and prefer activities that involve other children.

INITIATIVE, ENGAGEMENT, AND PERSISTENCE

	1–2 years	2–3 years	3–4 years	4–5 years	5–6 years
Decision-Making	Indicates preferences nonverbally or with simple language (e.g., points to an apple and pushes banana away).	Makes choices (e.g., food, clothes, toys, activities) based on preferences, sometimes in opposition to adult choices (e.g., child says, "No jacket. Want hat!").	Becomes increasingly deliberate when choosing preferred activities and companions (e.g., child says, "I want to play at Jeremy's house today.").	Further expands areas of decision-making (e.g., child may say, "This morning I'm going to work on my Lego building.").	Deliberates and weighs choices (e.g., may spend a long time thinking about whether to go to the store with mom or to stay home and help dad).

Attention	Focuses attention on interesting sights or sounds, often in shared experiences with adults (e.g., sits on father's lap looking at a picture book).	Increases ability to sustain attention, especially when it directly influences an activity (e.g., repeatedly stacks blocks and knocks them down).	Is able to focus attention for longer periods of time, even with distractions or interruptions, as long as the activity is age-appropriate and of interest (e.g., can repeatedly solve and dump out a wooden puzzle, even with the TV on in the background).	Has an increased ability to focus attention, and can ignore more distractions and interruptions (e.g., at preschool, can focus on a drawing even when other children are nearby; might say, "I'll play with you later. I want to finish this.").	Can maintain focus on a project for a sustained period of time (e.g., spends a rainy day building a complicated fort out of chairs and blankets, complete with props and signs). Is able to return to an activity after being interrupted.
Persistence and Task Completion	Shows pleasure in completing simple tasks (e.g., drops clothespins into a bucket and smiles and claps when all are inside).	Completes self-chosen, short-term, concrete tasks. Practices an activity many times to gain mastery (e.g., repeatedly moves magnetic letters on and off the refrigerator).	Persists with a wider variety of tasks, activities, and experiences. Keeps working to complete a task even if it is moderately difficult (e.g., persists with a somewhat challenging wooden puzzle).	Is increasingly able to complete tasks, even those that are longer-term and less-concrete (e.g., keeping track of the days until his or her birthday on a calendar). Has greater ability to set goals and follow a plan (e.g., child says, "I'm going to pick up all these branches," and then works until it is done).	Persists in longer-term or complex projects, with supervision. Can return to projects begun the previous day. Uses self-talk and other strategies to help finish difficult tasks and assignments from adults (e.g., a school project to make an alphabet book).
Self-Help and Independence in Learning	Increasingly tries to help with self-care activities (e.g., feeding, undressing, grooming). When reading with adults, may want to hold the book or try to turn the pages. Collects information about the world using the senses.	Has a growing interest in and ability to perform routine tasks independently (e.g., puts napkins on the table before dinner).	Expands abilities to independently complete a range of self-help skills (e.g., feeding, undressing, grooming). May refuse adult assistance (e.g., tries over and over to pull on a sweater and pushes mom's hands away when she tries to help).	Increasingly makes independent choices and shows self-reliance (e.g., chooses clothes, feeds and dresses self).	Chooses and follows through on self-selected learning tasks. Shows interest and skill in more complex self-help skills (e.g., decides to learn to skate, zips jacket, prepares a snack).

CURIOSITY AND EAGERNESS TO LEARN

	1–2 years	2–3 years	3–4 years	4–5 years	5–6 years
Participation in Varied Experiences	Actively participates in a variety of sensory experiences (e.g., tastes, touches, pats, shakes).	Is able to participate in a broader array of experiences (e.g., exploring outdoor playground equipment, climbing on rocks, investigating contents of kitchen cabinets, paging through books), thanks to increased physical and cognitive skills.	Continues to seek and engage in sensory and other experiences (e.g., listens to stories, plays with friends, takes trips to the fire station).	Asks to participate in new experiences that he or she has observed or has heard of others participating in (e.g., says, "Jack goes fishing. Can I?").	Tries an even wider range of new experiences, both independently and with peers and adults (e.g., goes on a camping trip with grandparents, tries to learn to play piano like older brother). May deliberately take risks when learning new skills.
Questioning	May seek information from adults by pointing to an interesting object, and then giving a questioning look, making a vocal sound, and/or saying a single word. In the second half of the year, children will be able to combine words to ask simple questions (e.g., says, "What that?" or "Who coming?").	May ask many "why," "what," and "how" questions about a variety of sights, sounds, and experiences (e.g., asks, "Why mommy cry?").	Continues to ask numerous questions, which are becoming more verbally complex (e.g., asks, "How we get to Nana's house?").	Asks questions about future events, as well as about the here and now (e.g., asks, "When will we go to Sarah's house again?").	Asks higher-level questions (e.g., asks, "What would happen if we had no food?" or "Why was Raymond mad at me?").
Eagerness to Learn	Shows physical and vocal pleasure when exploring objects and other things. Finds pleasure in causing things to happen (e.g., picks up bells and rings them, then smiles broadly when each one sounds different).	Continues to show enthusiasm and pleasure in daily explorations. Enjoys solving simple problems (e.g., successfully puts on own hat after several tries, then happily jumps up and down).	Seeks out new challenges (e.g., tries to dress a doll or put together a new construction toy).	Starts to show more enthusiasm for learning letters, shapes, and numbers (e.g., while looking at a book with dad, points to a word that contains the letter "S" and says, "S! That's in my name! What is that word?").	Expands verbal and nonverbal enthusiasm for learning new things, including academic (e.g., reading, writing) and physical skills (e.g., riding a bike).

REASONING AND PROBLEM-SOLVING					
Flexibility and Resilience	Tries a variety of physical strategies to reach simple goals (e.g., when a cart gets stuck while being pushed through a door, he or she turns the cart a different way and tries again).	Becomes more systematic in using language and physical approaches to solve problems, but may become stuck on one solution (e.g., tries numerous strategies for nesting a set of cups of graduated sizes, but may keep pushing harder to get a large cup to fit into a smaller one).	Continues to become more flexible in problem-solving and thinking through alternatives (e.g., when trying to put on shoes, talks to self about what to do first. If the shoe won't easily go on one foot, he or she tries the other foot.).	More flexible and able to draw on varied resources in solving problems (e.g., tries to build a large structure with blocks, but the building keeps falling down. After several failed attempts, he or she tries making a larger base. May also look at how other children have made their buildings.).	Is increasingly able to think of possible solutions to problems. Can use varied and flexible approaches to solve longer-term or more abstract challenges (e.g., when planning to have friends over on a rainy day, thinks about how to deal with a limited space to play).
Help-Seeking	Uses gestures and (toward the end of the year) simple language to get help when "stuck" (e.g., extends arms toward grandfather and says, "Up Up!" when trying to get into large chair).	Continues to expand use of language to get help, but may refuse assistance even when needed (e.g., may say, "I need help!" when trying to get a little car into the garage, but then says, "Do it myself!" when help arrives).	Increasingly able to ask for help on challenging tasks (e.g., says, "Can you put Teddy's pants on?").	Seeks help from both adults and peers, and has a greater understanding of the kind of help that may be needed (e.g., says, "Can you hold this end of the string for me, so I can tie this?").	Analyzes complex problems more accurately to identify the type of help needed (e.g., says, "I think I know how to play this game, but I think you'll have to help me get started. Then I can do the rest.").
Thinking Skills	Discovers aspects of the physical world using early language skills and purposeful exploration with the senses (e.g., turns a plastic bucket over and over, raising and lowering the handle thoughtfully).	Grows in abilities to recognize and solve problems through active exploration, including trial and error (e.g., tries to get a large pillow into a small container by turning it this way and that; eventually folds up pillow so it fits).	Thinks more systematically. Benefits from conversations with adults and peers, as well as physical investigation.	Grows in ability to understand abstract concepts, especially when his or her thinking is supported by physical interaction with materials (e.g., systematically pours sand into measuring cups, then looks at and comments on amounts).	Continues to benefit from hands-on experiences to support more abstract thinking skills (e.g., makes a book about last summer's vacation trip, complete with sections for each place visited, drawings to illustrate, and labels written with adult help).

INVENTION AND IMAGINATION

	1–2 years	2–3 years	3–4 years	4–5 years	5–6 years
Pretending	Pretends one object is really another with simple physical substitutions (e.g., picks up a wooden block and holds it to his or her ear like a phone).	Engages in simple pretend play with familiar objects and situations (e.g., puts doll to bed and lays blanket over her).	Grows in ability to sustain pretend play with other children (e.g., plays in pretend kitchen with friend, serving "cookies"). Takes on familiar roles (e.g., mom or dad) in pretend play.	Engages in more sustained and complex pretend play (e.g., creates a long scenario with several other children, taking a pretend trip with many stops). Expands the roles acted out in pretend play. Is less dependent on realistic props.	Collaborates with other children in extended and complex pretend play, taking on more varied roles and situations (e.g., acts out roles of lions, hunters, rescuers, and other animals in a dramatic and sustained scenario).
Creative Approaches to Situations	Uses objects in new and unexpected ways (e.g., puts saucepan on head, laughs uproariously).	Expands use of objects, art materials, and toys in new and unexpected ways (e.g., takes bath towels out of a closet and drapes them over chairs, crumples up paper in interesting shapes when pasting onto cardboard).	Plays creatively with both language and objects. Expresses inventive ideas in an expanding set of situations (e.g., creates interesting scenes with small plastic animals; strings nonsense words together, "Mommy, nommy, sommy, tommy").	Offers creative, unusual ideas about how to do a task, how to make something, or how to get from one place to another (e.g., says, "I've got a great idea! Let's walk backwards to the kitchen!").	Offers increasingly creative, unusual ideas about how to do a task, how to make something, or how to get from one place to another (e.g., asks, "Let's use these old boxes to make a spaceship! Where's some paint?").

APPENDIX B

Action Planning Form

THE ACTION PLANNING FORM is aligned with the evidence-based "Tools to Support Positive Approaches to Learning" described in Part II of this book. To use the form, begin by reviewing the list of tools, checking off those that are your highest priorities for action. Then note the specific steps that may be needed to accomplish these priorities, using the book as a resource. It will be helpful also to list the kinds of resources you may need as you take these steps: These might be material resources, additional reading or other professional development in certain areas, individuals who can coach or mentor you, and so forth. Finally, there is space to record your progress over time.

You are welcome to make copies of the Action Planning Form for your own use or for students or colleagues. A free, printable version is also available for download at the Teachers College Press Web site: www.tcpress.com.

Good luck and thank you for your commitment to every child becoming a more enthusiastic and engaged learner.

❖ ACTION PLANNING FORM

Tools to strengthen children's positive approaches to learning	My priorities	Actions needed to accomplish priorities	Resources needed (people, professional development, materials, etc.)	Progress notes
1. TOOLS TO BUILD CLOSER RELATIONSHIPS WITH ALL CHILDREN				
Find everyday ways to strengthen personal connections with children				
Create a sense of community for children				
2. TOOLS TO FIND AND USE MORE EFFECTIVE CURRICULUM				
Analyze various curriculum models for their approaches-to-learning emphasis				
Adapt existing curriculum to strengthen its approaches-to-learning focus				
Find and consider using curriculum specifically targeted to approaches to learning				

3. TOOLS TO TEACH IN WAYS THAT PROMOTE CHILDREN'S POSITIVE APPROACHES TO LEARNING

Create classroom environments that promote enthusiasm and engagement			
Intentionally use teaching practices that are known to support positive approaches to learning			

4. TOOLS TO ASSESS CHILDREN'S APPROACHES TO LEARNING

Find familiar assessments that can also be used to assess approaches to learning			
Find and use more specialized assessments of approaches to learning			
Make plans to use the results of assessments to strengthen children's enthusiasm and engagement			

5. TOOLS THAT TAP THE POWER OF FAMILIES

Develop respectful, reciprocal relationships with all families			
Find ways to have focused conversations with families about approaches to learning			
Share practical ideas with families, so they can support their children's enthusiasm and engagement			

Tools to strengthen children's positive approaches to learning	My priorities	Actions needed to accomplish priorities	Resources needed (people, professional development, materials, etc.)	Progress notes
6. TOOLS TO CREATE CHANGE				
Develop a theory of change and a logic model to achieve systems-level changes that support children's approaches to learning				
Become involved in generating, finding, and using research on approaches to learning				
Create effective professional development to help early childhood practitioners understand and promote children's enthusiasm and engagement				
Advocate for policies and resources that will increase positive approaches to learning for all children				
Use insights from the new fields of knowledge utilization and implementation research to more effectively connect research on approaches to learning with policy and practice				

References

Anderson, A. A. (2004). *Theory of change as a tool for strategic planning: A report on early experiences.* The Aspen Institute. Retrieved February 25, 2008, from http://www.theory ofchange.org/tocII_final4.pdf

Arend, R., Gove, F. L., & Sroufe, L. A. (1979). Continuity of individual adaptation from infancy to kindergarten: A predictive study of ego-resiliency and curiosity in preschoolers. *Child Development, 50*(4), 950–959.

Aubrun, A., & Grady, J. (2002). *What kids need and what kids give back: A review of communications materials used by early childhood development advocates to promote school readiness and related issues.* Washington, DC: FrameWorks Institute. Retrieved February 25, 2008, from http://www.frameworksinstitute.org/products/CL-PackMats8191.pdf

Baratta-Lorton, M. B. (1978). *Workjobs II: Number activities for early childhood.* New York: Pearson Learning.

Barbarin, O. (2002). Ready or not! African American males in kindergarten. In B. Bowman (Ed.), *Love to read: Essays in developing and enhancing early literacy skills of African American children* (pp. 1–15). Washington, DC: National Black Child Development Institute.

Barnett, D. W., Bauer, A. M., Ehrhardt, K. E., Lentz, F. E., & Stollar, S. A. (1996). Keystone targets for changes: Planning for widespread positive consequences. *School Psychology Quarterly, 11*, 95–117.

Barrett, K. C., Morgan, G. A., & Maslin-Cole, C. (1993). Three studies on the development of mastery motivation in infancy and toddlerhood. In D. J. Messer (Ed.), *Mastery motivation in early childhood: Development, measurement, and social processes* (pp. 83–108). New York: Routledge.

Blair, C. (2002). School readiness as propensity for engagement: Integrating cognition and emotion in a neurobiological conceptualization of child functioning at school entry. *American Psychologist, 57*, 111–127.

Blair, C., Zelazo, P. D., & Greenberg, M. T. (2005). The measurement of executive function in young children. *Developmental Neuropsychology, 28*, 561–571.

Blinco, P. M. A. (1992). A cross-cultural study of task persistence of young children in Japan and the United States. *Journal of Cross-Cultural Psychology, 23*(3), 407–415.

Bluestein, J. (2001). *Creating emotionally safe schools: A guide for educators and parents.* Deerfield Beach, FL: Health Communications.

Bodrova, E., & Leong, D. J. (2007). *Tools of the Mind: The Vygotskian approach to early childhood education* (2nd ed.). New York: Prentice Hall.

Bogenschneider, K., & Gross, E. (2004). From ivory tower to state house: How youth theory can inform youth policy making. *Family Relations, 52*, 19–25.

Bogenschneider, K., Olson, J. R., Linney, K. D., & Mills, J. (2000). Connecting research and policymaking: Implications for theory and practice from the family impact seminars. *Family Relations, 49*, 327–339.

Bohn, C. M., Roehrig, A. D., & Pressley, M. (2004). The first days of school in the classrooms of two more effective and four less effective primary-grades teachers. *The Elementary School Journal, 104*(4), 269–287.

Bowman, B. T., Donovan, M. S., & Burns, M. S. (Eds.). (2001). *Eager to learn: Educating our preschoolers.* Committee on Early Childhood Pedagogy, National Research Council. Washington, DC: National Academies Press.

Bransford, J. D., Brown, A. L., & Cocking, R. R. (1999). *How people learn: Brain, mind, experience, and school.* Washington, DC: National Academies Press.

Bredekamp, S., & Copple, C. (Eds.). (1997). *Developmentally appropriate practice in early childhood programs.* Washington, DC: National Association for the Education of Young Children.

Bronfenbrenner, U. (1978). *The ecology of human development.* Cambridge: Harvard University Press.

Bronfenbrenner, U. (2000). The ecology of developmental processes. In W. Damon & R. M. Lerner (Eds.), *Handbook of child psychology: Vol. 1. Theoretical models of human development* (5th ed., pp. 993–1028). New York: Wiley.

Bronfenbrenner, U., & Morris, P. A. (2006). The bioecological model of human development. In W. Damon & R. M. Lerner (Eds.), *Handbook of child psychology: Vol. 1. Theoretical models of human development* (6th ed., pp. 793–828). New York: Wiley.

Brophy, J. E. (2004). *Motivating students to learn* (2nd ed.). Mahwah, NJ: Erlbaum.

Broussard, S. C., & Garrison, M. E. (2004). The relationship between classroom motivation and academic achievement in elementary-school-aged children. *Family and Consumer Sciences Research Journal, 33*(2), 106–120.

Burchinal, M. R., Peisner-Feinberg, E., Pianta, R. C., & Howes, C. (2002). Development of academic skills from preschool through second grade: Family and classroom predictors of developmental trajectories. *Journal of School Psychology, 40*(5), 415–436.

Buysse, V., & Wesley, P. W. (Eds.). (2005). *Evidence-based practice in the early childhood field.* Washington, DC: Zero to Three.

Cameron, C., McClelland, M., Connor, C., Jewkes, A., Farris, C., & Morrison, F. (in press). Touch Your Toes! Developing a behavioral measure of preschool self-regulation. *Early Childhood Research Quarterly.*

Carle, E. (1969). *The very hungry caterpillar.* New York: Penguin.

Casey, A. M., & McWilliam, R. A. (2007). The STARE: The Scale for Teachers' Assessment of Routines Engagement. *Young Exceptional Children, 11*(1), 2–15.

Center on the Social and Emotional Foundations for Early Learning. (2008). A pyramid model for supporting social and emotional competence in infants and young children. Nashville, TN: Vanderbilt University. Retrieved February 25, 2008, from http://www.vanderbilt.edu/csefel

Chalufour, I., & Worth, K. (2003). *Discovering nature with young children* (Young Scientist Series). St. Paul, MN: Redleaf Press.

Chalufour, I., & Worth, K. (2004). *Building structures with young children* (Young Scientist Series). St. Paul, MN: Redleaf Press.

Chalufour, I., & Worth, K. (2005). *Exploring water with young children* (Young Scientist Series). St. Paul, MN: Redleaf Press.

Chard, S. (1998). *The Project Approach: Making curriculum come alive* (Book 1). New York: Scholastic.

Chen, J. Q., & McNamee, G. (2007). *Bridging: Assessment for teaching and learning in early childhood classrooms.* Thousand Oaks, CA: Corwin Press.

Childs, G., & McKay, M. (2001). Boys starting school disadvantaged: Implications from teachers' ratings of behaviour and achievement in the first two years. *British Journal of Educational Psychology, 71*(2), 303–314.

Clifford, R. M., Barbarin, O., Chang, F., Early, D. M., Bryant, D., Howes, C., et al. (2005). What is pre-kindergarten? Characteristics of public pre-kindergarten programs. *Applied Developmental Science, 9*(3), 126–143.

Cohn, D. (2006). Jumping into the political fray: Academics and policy-making. *IRPP Policy Matters, 7*(3), 1–31.

Csikszentmihalyi, M. (1990). *Flow: The psychology of optimal experience.* New York: Harper and Row.

Curtis, D., & Carter, M. (2003). *Designs for living and learning: Transforming early childhood environments.* St. Paul, MN: Redleaf Press.

de Kruif, R. E. L., & McWilliam, R. A. (1999). Multivariate relationships among developmental age, global engagement, and observed child engagement. *Early Childhood Research Quarterly, 14*(4), 515–536.

de Kruif, R. E. L., McWilliam, R. A., Ridley, S. M., & Wakely, M. B. (2000). Classification of teachers' interaction behaviors in early childhood classrooms. *Early Childhood Research Quarterly, 15*(2), 247–268.

Delpit, L. (2006). *Other people's children: Cultural conflict in the classroom* (2nd ed.). New York: New Press.

Diffily, D., & Morrison, K. (1996). *Family-friendly communication for early childhood programs.* Washington, DC: National Association for the Education of Young Children.

Diffily, D., & Sassman, C. (2002). *Project-based learning with young children.* Portsmouth, NH: Heinemann.

Dilcher, A. F., & Hyson, M. (1997, April). *Influences on the activity engagement of young children with and without disabilities: Adult emotion and activity type.* Poster session presented at the biennial meeting of the Society for Research in Child Development, Washington, DC.

Division for Early Childhood. (2007). *Promoting positive outcomes for children with disabilities: Recommendations for curriculum, assessment, and program evaluation.* Missoula, MT: Author.

Dodge, D. T., & Bickart, T. S. (2002). How curriculum frameworks respond to developmental stages: Birth through age 8. In D. Rothenberg (Ed.), *Issues in early childhood education: Curriculum, teacher education, and dissemination of information. Proceedings of the Lilian Katz Symposium* (pp. 33–41). University of Illinois at Urbana-Champaign: Early Childhood and Parenting Collaborative.

Dodge, D. T., Colker, L. J., & Heroman, C. (2002). *The creative curriculum for preschool* (4th ed.). Washington, DC: Teaching Strategies.

Dolezal, S. E., Welsh, L. M., Pressley, M., & Vincent, M. (2003). How do grade-3 teachers motivate their students? *Elementary School Journal, 103,* 239–267.

Dweck, C. (2000). *Self-theories: Their role in motivation, personality, and development.* London: Taylor and Francis.

Early, D. M., Maxwell, K. L., Burchinal, M., Alva, S., Bender, R., Bryant, D., et al. (2007). Teachers' education, classroom quality, and young children's academic skills: Results from seven studies of preschool programs. *Child Development, 78*(2), 558–580.

Educators for Social Responsibility. (2007). *Twenty kinds of class meetings.* Cambridge, MA: Author. Retrieved February 25, 2008, from http://www.ethicsed.org/consulting/meeting ideas.htm

Edwards, C. P., Gandini, L., & Forman, G. (Eds.). (1998). *The hundred languages of children: The Reggio Emilia approach—Advanced reflections* (2nd ed.). Greenwich, CT: Ablex.

Elicker, J., & Mathur, S. (1997). What do they do all day? Comprehensive evaluation of a full-day kindergarten. *Early Childhood Research Quarterly, 12*(4), 459–480.

Elliot, A. J., & Dweck, C. S. (Eds.). (2005). *Handbook of competence and motivation.* New York: Guilford Press.

Epstein, A. (2006). *The intentional teacher: Choosing the best strategies for young children's learning.* Washington, DC: National Association for the Education of Young Children.

Erikson, E. H. (1950). *Childhood and society*. New York: Norton.

Falk, B., & Blumenreich, M. (2005). *The power of questions: A guide to teacher and student research*. Portsmouth, NH: Heinemann.

Fantuzzo, J. W., Gadsden, V., & McDermott, P. (2008, June). *Evidence-Based Program for the Integration of Curricula (EPIC)*. Paper to be presented at Head Start's Ninth National Research Conference, Washington, DC.

Fantuzzo, J., & McDermott, P. (2008, June). *Learning-in-time and teaching-to-learn: The unique contribution of learning behaviors to early school success*. Invited paper to be presented in the "Fostering Active Engagement in Learning" Symposium (Clancy Blair, Symposium Chair) at Head Start's Ninth National Research Conference, Washington, DC.

Fantuzzo, J., Perry, M. A., & McDermott, P. (2004). Preschool approaches to learning and their relationship to other relevant classroom competencies for low-income children. *School Psychology Quarterly, 19*(3), 212–230.

Fixsen, D. L., Naoom, S. F., Blase, K. A., Friedman, R. M., & Wallace, F. (2005). *Implementation research: A synthesis of the literature*. Tampa: University of South Florida, Louis de la Parte Florida Mental Health Institute, The National Implementation Research Network.

Fox, L., Dunlap, G., Hemmeter, M. L., Joseph, G., & Strain, P. (2003). The teaching pyramid: A model for supporting social competence and preventing challenging behavior in young children. *Young Children, 58*(4), 48–53.

Frank Porter Graham Child Development Center. (2001). *The quality and engagement study. Final report* (R. A. McWilliam, Principal Investigator). Chapel Hill, NC: Author.

Frede, E., & Ackerman, D. J. (2007, March). Preschool curriculum decision-making: Dimensions to consider. *NIEER Preschool Policy Brief*, Issue 12. New Brunswick, NJ: National Institute for Early Education Research. Retrieved February 25, 2008, from http://nieer.org/resources/policybriefs/12.pdf

Fromberg, D. P. (1992). Implementing the full-day kindergarten. *Principal, 71*(5), 26–28.

Furrer, C., & Skinner, E. A. (2003). Sense of relatedness as a factor in children's academic engagement and performance. *Journal of Educational Psychology, 95*(1), 148–162.

Gandini, L., Hill, L., Cadwell, L., & Schwall, C. (2005). *In the spirit of the studio: Learning from the atelier of Reggio Emilia*. New York: Teachers College Press.

Gardner, H. (1993). *Multiple intelligences: The theory in practice*. New York: Basic Books.

George, J., & Greenfield, D. B. (2005). Examination of a structured problem-solving flexibility task for assessing approaches to learning in young children: Relation to teacher ratings and children's achievement. *Applied Developmental Psychology, 26*(1), 69–84.

Goffin, S. G., & Wilson, C. S. (2001). *Curriculum models and early childhood education: Appraising the relationship* (2nd ed.). Upper Saddle River, NJ: Prentice Hall.

Gottfried, A. E. (1990). Academic intrinsic motivation in young elementary school children. *Journal of Educational Psychology, 82*(3), 525–538.

Gottfried, A. E., Fleming, J. S., & Gottfried, A. W. (1994). Role of parental motivational practices in children's academic intrinsic motivation and achievement. *Journal of Educational Psychology, 86*(1), 104–113.

Gottfried, A. E., Fleming, J. S., & Gottfried, A. W. (1998). The role of cognitively stimulating home environment in children's academic intrinsic motivation: A longitudinal study. *Child Development, 69*(5), 1448–1460.

Graham, S., & Taylor, A. (2002). Ethnicity, gender, and the development of achievement values. In A. Wigfield & J. S. Eccles (Eds.), *Development of achievement motivation* (pp. 121–146). San Diego, CA: Academic Press.

Graves, M. (1997). *100 small group experiences: The teacher's idea book 3*. Ypsilanti, MI: High/Scope Press.

Greenfield, P. M., Quiroz, B., & Raeff, C. (2000). Cross-cultural conflict and harmony in the social construction of the child. In S. Harkness, C. Raeff, & C. M. Super (Eds.), *Variabil-*

ity in the social construction of the child: Vol. 87. New directions for child and adolescent development (pp. 93–108). San Francisco: Jossey-Bass.

Greenman, J. (1987). *Caring spaces, learning places: Children's environments that work.* Bellevue, WA: Exchange Press.

Greenman, J. (2005). Places for childhood in the 21st century: A conceptual framework. Beyond the Journal: *Young Children* on the Web. Retrieved February 25, 2008, from http://www.journal.naeyc.org/btj/200505/01Greenman.pdf

Gresham, F. M., & Elliott, S. N. (1990). *Social Skills Rating System.* Circle Pines, MN: American Guidance Service.

Grolnick, W., & Ryan, R. (1989). Parental styles associated with children's self-regulation and competence in school. *Journal of Educational Psychology, 81*(2), 143–154.

Guthrie, J. T., & Alvermann, D. E. (Eds.). (1999). *Engaged reading: Processes, practices, and policy implications* (Language and Literacy Series). New York: Teachers College Press.

Guthrie, J. T., & Wigfield, A. (2000). Engagement and motivation in reading. In M. L. Kamil, P. B. Mosenthal, P. D. Pearson, & R. Barr (Eds.), *Handbook of reading research* (Vol. 3, pp. 403–422). New York: Erlbaum.

Gutiérrez, K., & Rogoff, B. (2003). Cultural ways of learning: Individual traits or repertoires of practice. *Educational Researcher, 32*(5), 19–25.

Hanson, M. J., & Lynch, E. W. (2003). *Understanding families: Approaches to diversity, disability, and risk.* Baltimore: Brookes.

Harris, J. (2001). Logic model basics. Out-of-School Time Issue #2. *The Evaluation Exchange, 7*(2). Retrieved February 25, 2008, from http://www.gse.harvard.edu/hfrp/eval/issue17/html/spotlight2.html

Harter, S. (1996). Teacher and classmate influences on scholastic motivation, self-esteem, and level of voice in adolescents. In J. Juvonen & K. R. Wentzel (Eds.), *Social motivation: Understanding children's school adjustment* (pp. 11–42). Cambridge, UK: Cambridge University Press.

Head Start Bureau. (2001). Head Start Child Outcomes Framework. *Head Start Bulletin* 70. Washington, DC: Department of Health and Human Services, Administration for Children and Families. Retrieved February 25, 2008, from http://www.headstartinfo.org/pdf/im00_18a.pdf

Helm, J. H., Berg, S., & Scranton, P. (2004). *Teaching your child to love learning.* New York: Teachers College Press.

Helm, J., & Katz, L. (2001). *Young investigators: The Project Approach in the early years.* New York: Teachers College Press.

High/Scope Educational Research Foundation. (2003). *High/Scope Preschool Child Observation Record (COR).* Ypsilanti, MI: High/Scope Press.

Hirsh-Pasek, K., Hyson, M., & Rescorla, L. (1990). Academic environments in preschool: Do they pressure or challenge young children? *Early Education and Development, 1*(6), 401–423.

Hohman, M., & Weikart, D. P. (1995). *Educating young children: Active learning practices for preschool and child care programs.* Ypsilanti, MI: High/Scope Press.

Howell, N. (1999). Cooking-up a learning community with corn, beans, and rice. *Young Children, 54*(5), 36–38.

Howes, C., & Ritchie, S. (2002). *A matter of trust: Connecting teachers and learners in the early childhood classroom.* New York: Teachers College Press.

Hughes, J. N., Zhang, D., & Hill, C. R. (2006). Peer assessments of normative and individual teacher–student support predict social acceptance and engagement among low-achieving children. *Journal of School Psychology, 43*(6), 447–463.

Huston, A. C. (2005). Connecting the science of child development to public policy. *Social Policy Reports, 19*(4), 3–18.

Hyson, M. (Ed.). (2003). Preparing early childhood professionals: NAEYC's standards for programs. Washington, DC: National Association for the Education of Young Children.

Hyson, M. (2004). *The emotional development of young children: Building an emotion-centered curriculum* (2nd ed.). New York: Teachers College Press.

Hyson, M. (2007). Curriculum. In R. New & M. Cochran (Eds.), *Early childhood education: An international encyclopedia* (Vol. 1, pp. 176–181). New York: Greenwood Press.

Hyson, M., & Biggar, H. (2005). NAEYC's standards for early childhood professional preparation: Getting from here to there. In M. Zaslow & I. Martinez-Beck (Eds.), *Critical issues in early childhood professional development* (pp. 283–308). Baltimore: Brookes.

Hyson, M., Copple, C., & Jones, J. (2006). Early childhood development and education. In K. A. Renninger & I. Sigel (Eds.), *Handbook of child psychology: Vol. 4. Child psychology in practice* (pp. 3–47). New York: Wiley.

Hyson, M., Tomlinson, H. B., & Lutton, A. (2007, March). Quality of early childhood teacher preparation: A moderating variable in the relationship between teachers' education and children's outcomes? Paper presented at the biennial meeting of the Society for Research in Child Development, Boston, MA.

Izard, C. E., & Ackerman, B. P. (2000). Motivational, organizational, and regulatory functions of discrete emotions. In M. Lewis & J. M. Haviland-Jones (Eds.), *Handbook of emotions* (2nd ed., pp. 253–264). New York: Guilford.

Jones, N. P. (2005). Big Jobs: Planning for competence. *Young Children, 60*(2), 86–93.

Kagan, S. L., Moore, E., & Bredekamp, S. (Eds.). (1995). *Reconsidering children's early learning and development: Toward common views and vocabulary* (Report of the National Education Goals Panel, Goal 1 Technical Planning Group, No. ED 391 576). Washington, DC: U.S. Government Printing Office.

Kaiser, B., & Rasminsky, J. S. (2003). *Challenging behavior in young children: Understanding, preventing, and responding effectively* (2nd ed.). Boston: Allyn & Bacon.

Katz, L. G. (1991). Pedagogical issues in early childhood education. In S. L. Kagan (Ed.), *The care and education of America's young children: Obstacles and opportunities. Ninetieth Yearbook of the National Society for the Study of Education. Part I* (pp. 50–68). Chicago: University of Chicago Press.

Katz, L. G. (1993). *Dispositions: Definitions and implications for early childhood practices.* Urbana, IL: ERIC Clearinghouse on Elementary and Early Childhood Education.

Katz, L. G. (1995). Dispositions in early childhood education. In L. G. Katz (Ed.), *Talks with teachers of young children: A collection* (pp. 47–69). Norwood, NJ: Ablex.

Katz, L., & Chard, S. (2000). *Engaging children's minds: The project approach* (2nd ed.). Stamford, CT: Ablex.

Kelly, J., & Barnard, K. (1999). Parent education within a relationship-focused model. *Topics in Early Childhood Special Education, 19*(3), 151–157.

Kendall, J. S., & Marzano, R. J. (1995). *The systematic identification and articulation of content standards and benchmarks: Update.* Washington, DC: U.S. Government Printing Office.

Kessler, S. A., & Swadener, B. B. (Eds.). (1992). *Reconceptualizing the early childhood curriculum: Beginning the dialogue.* New York: Teachers College Press.

Keyser, J. (2006). *From parents to partners: Building a family-centered early childhood program.* St. Paul, MN: Redleaf Press.

Kirschen, M. (2005). *Thirty ways to show students you care!* Wallingford, CT: Education World. Retrieved February 25, 2008, from http://www.education-world.com/a_curr/curr286.html

Klein, L., & Knitzer, J. (2006). *Effective preschool curricula and teaching strategies* (Pathways to Early School Success, Issue Brief No. 2). New York: National Center for Children in Poverty. Retrieved March 15, 2008, from http://www.nccp.org/publications/pdf/text_668.pdf

Kohn, A. (1993). Choices for children: Why and how to let students decide. *Phi Delta Kappan, 75*, 8–20.

Koralek, D. (Ed.). (2007). *Spotlight on young children and families.* Washington, DC: National Association for the Education of Young Children.

Kritchevsky, S., Prescott, E., & Walling, L. (1977). *Planning environments for young children: Physical space* (2nd ed.). Washington, DC: National Association for the Education of Young Children.

Kumar, R., Gheen, M. H., & Kaplan, A. (2002). Goal structures in the learning environment and students' disaffection from learning and schooling. In C. Midgley (Ed.), *Goals, goal structures, and patterns of adaptive learning* (pp. 143–174). Mahwah, NJ: Erlbaum.

Ladson-Billings, G. (1995). Toward a theory of culturally relevant pedagogy. *American Education Research Journal, 32*(3), 465–491.

Ladson-Billings, G. (1997). *The dreamkeepers: Successful teachers of African American children.* San Francisco: Jossey-Bass.

LeBuffe, P. A., & Naglieri, J. A. (1999). *The Devereux Early Childhood Assessment.* Lewisville, NC: Kaplan Press.

Levin, D. E. (2003). *Teaching young children in violent times: Building a peaceable classroom* (2nd ed.). Cambridge, MA: Educators for Social Responsibility.

Lewis, C. R., Schaps, E., & Watson, M. (1995). Beyond the pendulum: Creating challenging and caring schools. *Phi Delta Kappan, 76*(7), 547–554.

Li-Grining, C., Madison-Boyd, S., Jones-Lewis, D., Smallwood, K. M., Sardin, L., Metzger, M. W., Jones, S. M., & Raver, C. C. (2007, March). *Implementing a classroom-based intervention in the "real world": The role of teachers' psychosocial stressors.* Paper presented at the biennial meeting of the Society for Research in Child Development, Boston, MA.

Lynch, E. W., & Hanson, M. J. (Eds.). (2004). *Developing cross-cultural competence: A guide for working with children and their families* (3rd ed.). Baltimore: Brookes.

Mahone, E. M., Pillion, J. P., Hoffman, J., Hiemenz, J. R., & Denckla, M. B. (2005). Construct validity of the auditory continuous performance test for preschoolers. *Developmental Neuropsychology, 27,* 11–33.

Marzano, R. J. (2007). *The art and science of teaching.* Alexandria, VA: Association for Supervision and Curriculum Development.

McCabe, M. A. (2007). Sharing knowledge for policy: The role of organizations as knowledge brokers. In E. Banister, B. Leadbeater, A. Marshall, & T. Riecken (Eds.), *Community-based approaches to knowledge translation.* Manuscript in preparation.

McClelland, M. M., Acock, A. C., & Morrison, F. J. (2006). The impact of kindergarten learning-related skills on academic trajectories at the end of elementary school. *Early Childhood Research Quarterly, 21*(4), 471–490.

McClelland, M. M., Cameron, C. E., Connor, C. M., Farris, C. L., Jewkes, A. M., & Morrison, F. J. (2007). Links between behavioral regulation and preschoolers' literacy, vocabulary, and math skills. *Developmental Psychology, 43,* 947–959.

McClelland, M. M., & Morrison, F. J. (2003). The emergence of learning-related social skills in preschool children. *Early Childhood Research Quarterly, 18*(2), 206–224.

McDermott, P. A., Leigh, N. M., & Perry, M. A. (2002). Evaluation and assessment: Development and validation of the Preschool Learning Behaviors Scale. *Psychology in the Schools, 39*(4), 353–365.

McTaggart, J. A., Frijters, J. C., & Barron, R. W. (2005, April). *Children's early interest in reading and math: A longitudinal study of motivation and academic skills.* Poster session presented at the biennial meeting of the Society for Research in Child Development, Atlanta, GA.

McWayne, C. M., Fantuzzo, J. W., & McDermott, P. A. (2004). Preschool competency in context: An investigation of the unique contribution of child competencies to early academic success. *Developmental Psychology, 40*(4), 633–645.

McWilliam, R. A. (1998). *Engagement Check II*. Chapel Hill: Frank Porter Graham Child Development Center, University of North Carolina at Chapel Hill.

McWilliam, R. A., & Casey, A. M. (2007). *Engagement of every child in the preschool classroom*. Baltimore: Brookes.

McWilliam, R. A., Scarborough, A. A., & Kim, H. (2003). Adult interactions and child engagement. *Early Education and Development, 14*(1), 7–27.

McWilliam, R. A., Trivette, C. M., & Dunst, C. J. (1985). Behavior engagement as a measure of the efficacy of early intervention. *Analysis and Intervention in Developmental Disabilities, 5*(1–2), 59–71.

Meisels, S. J. (1999). Assessing readiness. In R. C. Pianta & M. J. Cox (Eds.), *The transition to kindergarten* (pp. 39–66). Baltimore: Brookes.

Meisels, S. J., Jablon, J. R., Marsden, D. B., Dichtelmiller, M. L., & Dorfman, A. B. (2001). *The work sampling system* (4th ed.). New York: Pearson Learning Group.

Meisels, S. J., Marsden, D. B., Dombro, A. L., Weston, D. R., & Jewkes, A. M. (2003). *The Ounce Scale*. Upper Saddle River, NJ: Pearson.

Michigan Department of Education Early Childhood Programs. (1999). *A guide to home visits*. Lansing, MI: Author. Retrieved February 25, 2008, from http://www.michigan.gov/documents/Guide_to_Home_Visits_44583_7.pdf

Midgley, C. (Ed.). (2002). *Goals, goal structures, and patterns of adaptive learning*. Mahwah, NJ: Erlbaum.

Montessori, M. (1964). *The Montessori method*. New York: Schocken Books.

Montessori, M. (1995). *The absorbent mind*. New York: Henry Holt & Co.

Morrison, F. J. (Discussant). (2007, March). *Contemporary perspectives on children's engagement in learning*. Symposium presented at the biennial meeting of the Society for Research in Child Development, Boston, MA.

National Association for the Education of Young Children. (2005a). *Screening and assessment of young English-language learners* (Supplement to the NAEYC and NAECS/SDE Joint Position Statement on Early Childhood Curriculum, Assessment, and Program Evaluation). Retrieved February 25, 2008, from http://www.naeyc.org/about/positions/pdf/ELL_Supplement_Shorter_Version.pdf

National Association for the Education of Young Children. (2005b). *NAEYC early childhood program standards and accreditation criteria: The mark of quality in early childhood education*. Washington, DC: Author.

National Association for the Education of Young Children. (2006). Resources for supporting and involving families in meaningful ways. *Young Children 61*(1), 61–63. Retrieved February 25, 2008, from http://www.journal.naeyc.org/btj/200601/FamilyResourcesBTJ.pdf

National Association for the Education of Young Children. (2008). *NAEYC position statement on developmentally appropriate practice in early childhood programs serving children from birth through age 8*. Washington, DC: Author.

National Association for the Education of Young Children & National Association of Early Childhood Specialists in State Departments of Education. (2002). *Early learning standards: Creating the conditions for success. Joint position statement*. Retrieved February 25, 2008, from http://www.naeyc.org/about/positions/early_learning_standards.asp

National Association for the Education of Young Children & National Association of Early Childhood Specialists in State Departments of Education. (2003). *Early childhood curriculum, assessment, and program evaluation: Building an effective, accountable system in programs for children birth through age 8. Joint position statement*. Retrieved February 25, 2008, from http://www.naeyc.org/about/positions/pdf/CAPEexpand.pdf

National Center for Education Statistics. (2002). *Children's reading and mathematics achievement in kindergarten and first grade*. Washington, DC: Author. Retrieved February 25, 2008, from http://nces.ed.gov/pubs2002/kindergarten/24.asp?nav=4

National Center for Education Statistics. (n.d.). *Early Childhood Longitudinal Study—Kindergarten (ECLS-K)*. Washington, DC: Author. Retrieved March 15, 2008, from http://nces.ed.gov/ecls

National Council of Teachers of Mathematics. (2000). *Principles and standards for school mathematics*. Reston, VA: Author.

National Council of Teachers of Mathematics. (2006). *Curriculum focal points for prekindergarten through grade 8 mathematics: A quest for coherence*. Reston, VA: Author.

National Education Goals Panel. (1991). *The National Education Goals report: Building a nation of learners, 1991*. Washington, DC: U.S. Government Printing Office.

National Education Goals Panel. (1997). *Getting a good start in school*. Washington, DC: U.S. Government Printing Office.

National Institute of Child Health and Human Development Early Child Care Research Network. (2005). A day in third grade: A large-scale study of classroom quality and teacher and student behavior. *The Elementary School Journal, 105*(3), 305–323.

National Research Council. Committee on Increasing High School Students' Engagement and Motivation to Learn. (2003). *Engaging schools: Fostering high school students' motivation to learn*. Washington, DC: National Academies Press.

Neuman, S. B., & Roskos, K. (2005). The state of state prekindergarten standards. *Early Childhood Research Quarterly, 20*(2), 125–145.

Northwest Education Collaborative. (2001). *A caring community of learners: Creating a protective shield*. Portland, OR: Northwest Regional Educational Laboratory. Retrieved February 25, 2008, from http://www.nwrel.org/cfc/frc/beyus7.html

Ogbu, J. (1985). Cultural ecology of competence among inner-city Blacks. In M. B. Spencer, G. K. Brookins, & W. R. Allen (Eds.), *Beginnings: The social and affective development of Black children* (pp. 45–66). Hillsdale, NJ: Erlbaum.

Olson, M., & Hyson, M. (2005). Professional development: NAEYC explores parental perspectives on early childhood education. *Young Children, 60*(3), 66–68.

Organizational Research Services. (2004). *Theory of change: A practical tool for action, results, and learning*. Prepared for the Annie E. Casey Foundation. Retrieved February 25, 2008, from http://www.organizationalresearch.com/publications/aecf_theory_of_change_manual.pdf

Pewewardy, C., & Hammer, P. C. (2003). Culturally responsive teaching for American Indian students. *ERIC Digest ED482325*. Urbana, IL: ERIC Clearinghouse on Rural Education and Small Schools. Retrieved March 15, 2008, from http://www.eric.ed.gov:80/ERICDocs/data/ericdocs2sql/content_storage_01/0000019b/80/1b/8b/07.pdf

Phillips, D., & Adams, G. (2001). Child care and our youngest children. *The Future of Children, 11*(1), 34–51.

Piaget, J. (1962). *Play, dreams and imitation in childhood*. New York: Norton.

Pianta, R. C. (2000). *Enhancing relationships between children and teachers*. Washington, DC: American Psychological Association.

Pianta, R., Howes, C., Burchinal, M., Bryant, D., Clifford, R. M., Early, D. M., et al. (2005). Features of pre-kindergarten programs, classrooms, and teachers: Prediction of observed classroom quality and teacher–child interactions. *Applied Developmental Science, 9*(3), 144–159.

Pletcher, L. C., & McBride, S. (2004). *Family centered services: Guiding principles and practices for delivery of family centered services*. Developed jointly for Iowa's Early ACCESS and Project SCRIPT. Retrieved February 25, 2008, from http://www.extension.iastate.edu/culture/files/FamlCntrdSrvc.pdf

Powell, D. (2006). Families and early childhood interventions. In K. A. Renninger & I. Sigel (Eds.), *Handbook of child psychology: Vol. 4. Child psychology in practice* (pp. 548–591). New York: Wiley.

Project Zero & Reggio Children. (2001). *Making learning visible: Children as individual and group learners*. Reggio Emilia, Italy: Reggio Children.

Quintero, E. (1999). The new faces of Head Start: Learning from culturally diverse families. *Early Education and Development, 10*(4), 475–497.

Raver, C. C., Blackburn, E. K., Bancroft, M., & Torp, N. (1999). Relations between effective emotional self-regulation, attentional control, and low-income preschoolers' social competence with peers. *Early Education and Development, 10*(3), 333–350.

Ready, D. D., LoGerfo, L. F., Burkam, D. T., & Lee, V. E. (2005). Explaining girls' advantage in kindergarten literacy learning: Do classroom behaviors make a difference? *Elementary School Journal, 106*(1), 21–38.

Reeves, D. B. (2002). *The leader's guide to standards: A blueprint for educational equity and excellence.* San Francisco: Jossey-Bass.

Renninger, K. A. (2000). Individual interest and its implications for understanding intrinsic motivation. In C. Sansone and J. M. Harackiewicz (Eds.), *Intrinsic and extrinsic motivation: The search for optimal motivation and performance* (pp. 373–404). San Diego, CA: Academic Press.

Renninger, K. A., & Hidi, S. (2002). Student interest and achievement: Developmental issues raised by a case study. In A. Wigfield & J. S. Eccles (Eds.), *Development of achievement motivation* (pp. 173–195). New York: Academic Press.

Renninger, K. A., Hidi, S., & Krapp, A. (Eds.). (1992). *The role of interest in learning and development.* Hillsdale, NJ: Erlbaum.

Rider, R. J. (1997). On the nature of cognitive style. *Educational Psychology, 17*(1,2), 29–49.

Ridley, S. M., McWilliam, R. A., & Oates, C. S. (2000). Observed engagement as an indicator of child care program quality. *Early Education and Development, 11*(2), 133–146.

Rimm-Kaufman, S. E., La Paro, K. M., Downer, J. T., & Pianta, R. C. (2005). The contribution of classroom setting and quality of instruction to children's behavior in kindergarten classrooms. *Elementary School Journal, 105*(4), 377–394.

Robinson, A., & Stark, D. R. (2005). *Advocates in action: Making a difference for young children* (Rev. ed.). Washington, DC: National Association for the Education of Young Children.

Rogoff, B. (2003). The cultural nature of human development. New York: Oxford University Press.

Rothbart, M. K., & Bates, J. E. (2006). Temperament. In N. Eisenberg (Ed.), *Handbook of child psychology: Vol. 3. Social, emotional, and personality development* (pp. 99–166). New York: Wiley.

Rothbart, M. K., Sheese, B. E., & Posner, M. (2007). Executive function and effortful control: Linking temperament, brain networks, and genes. *Child Development Perspectives, 1*(1), 2–7.

Rouse, H., & Fantuzzo, J. (2008). Competence motivation in Head Start: An early childhood link to learning. Peer assisted learning strategies. In C. Hudley and A. Gottfried (Eds.), *Academic motivation and the culture of schooling.* New York: Oxford University Press.

Sagor, R. (2004). *The action research guidebook: A four-step process for educators and school teams.* Thousand Oaks, CA: Corwin Press.

Sandall, S. R., McLean, M., & Smith, B. (2000). *DEC recommended practices in early intervention/early childhood special education.* Longmont, CO: Sopris West.

Sandall, S. R., & Schwartz, I. S. (2002). *Building blocks for teaching preschoolers with special needs.* Baltimore: Brookes.

Schiefele, U., Krapp, A., & Winteler, A. (1992). Interest as a predictor of academic achievement: A meta-analysis of research. In K. A. Renninger, S. B. Hidi, & A. Krapp (Eds.), *The role of interest in learning and development* (pp. 183–212). Hillsdale, NJ: Erlbaum.

Schweder, R. A., Goodnow, J. J., Hatano, G., LeVine, R. A., Markus, H., & Miller, P. J. (2006). The cultural psychology of development: One mind, many mentalities. In W. Damon & R. M. Lerner (Eds.), *Handbook of child psychology: Vol. 1. Theoretical models of human development* (pp. 716–792). New York: Wiley.

Scott-Little, C., Kagan, S. L., & Frelow, V. S. (2005). *Inside the content: The breadth and depth of early learning standards.* Greensboro, NC: SERVE Center. Retrieved February 25, 2008, from http://www.serve.org/_downloads/publications/insidecontentes.pdf

Scott-Little, C., Lesko, J., Martella, J., & Milburn, P. (2007). Early learning standards: Results from a national survey to document trends in state-level policies and practices. *Early Childhood Research and Practice, 9*(1). Retrieved March 15, 2008, from http://ecrp.uiuc.edu/v9n1/little.html

Seefeldt, C. (Ed.). (1999). *The early childhood curriculum: Current findings in theory and practice* (3rd ed.). New York: Teachers College Press.

Shonkoff, J. P. (2000). Science, policy, and practice: Three cultures in search of a shared mission. *Child Development, 71,* 181–187.

Shonkoff, J. P., & Phillips, D. A. (2000). *From neurons to neighborhoods: The science of early childhood development.* Washington, DC: National Academy Press.

Stipek, D. (2002). *Motivation to learn: Integrating theory and practice* (4th ed.). Boston: Allyn & Bacon.

Stipek, D., Feiler, R., Daniels, D., & Milburn, S. (1995). Effects of different instructional approaches on young children's achievement and motivation. *Child Development, 66*(1), 209–223.

Stipek, D., & Seal, K. (2001). *Motivated minds: Raising children to love learning.* New York: Holt.

Torrence, M., & Chattin-McNichols, J. (2000). Montessori education today. In J. L. Roopnarine & J. E. Johnson (Eds.), *Approaches to early childhood education* (3rd ed., pp. 191–219). Upper Saddle River, NJ: Prentice Hall.

Turner, L. A., & Johnson, B. (2003). A model of mastery motivation for at-risk preschoolers. *Journal of Educational Psychology, 95*(3), 495–505.

U.S. Department of Education. The National Commission on Excellence in Education. (1983). *A nation at risk: The imperative for educational reform.* Washington, DC: Author.

Vance, E., & Weaver, P. J. (2002). *Class meetings: Young children solving problems together.* Washington, DC: National Association for the Education of Young Children.

Vinovskis, M. A. (1995). School readiness and early childhood education. In D. Ravitch and M. A. Vinovskis (Eds.), *Learning from the past: What history teaches us about school reform* (pp. 243–264). Baltimore: Johns Hopkins University Press.

Vygotsky, L. S. (1978). *Mind and society: The development of higher mental process.* Cambridge, MA: Harvard University Press. (Original work published 1930, 1933, 1935)

Waters, E., Wippman, J., & Sroufe, L. A. (1979). Attachment, positive affect, and competence in the peer group: Two studies in construct validation. *Child Development, 50*(3), 821–829.

Weiss, H. B., Caspe, M., & Lopez, M. E. (2006). Family involvement in early childhood education. *Family Involvement Makes a Difference, 1.* Retrieved February 25, 2008, from http://www.gse.harvard.edu/hfrp/content/projects/fine/resources/research/earlychildhood.pdf

Whitin, P. (2001). Kindness in a jar. *Young Children, 56*(5), 18–22.

Wigfield, A., & Eccles, J. S. (Eds.). (2002). *Development of achievement motivation.* San Diego, CA: Academic Press.

Wigfield, A., Eccles, J. S., Schiefele, U., Roeser, R. W., & Davis-Kean, P. (2006). Development of achievement motivation. In W. Damon, R. M. Lerner, & N. Eisenberg (Vol. Ed.), *Handbook of child psychology: Vol. 3. Social, emotional, and personality development* (6th ed., pp. 933–1002). New York: Wiley.

Wigfield, A., & Tonks, S. (2004). The development of motivation for reading and how it is influenced by CORI. In J. T. Guthrie, A. Wigfield, & K. C. Perencevich (Eds.), *Motivating reading comprehension: Concept-oriented reading instruction* (pp. 249–272). Mahwah, NJ: Erlbaum.

Winton, P. J., McCollum, J. A., & Catlett, C. (Eds.). (2007). *Practical approaches to early childhood professional development: Evidence, strategies, and resources.* Washington, DC: Zero to Three.

Zaslow, M., & Martinez-Beck, I. (Eds.). (2005). *Critical issues in early childhood professional development.* Baltimore: Brookes.

Zelazo, P. D., Müller, U., Frye, D., & Marcovitch, S. (2003). The development of executive function in early childhood. *Monographs of the Society for Research in Child Development, 68*(3, Serial No. 274).

Index

Page numbers in *italics* refer to figures and tables.

◆ About the Author

MARILOU HYSON, PH.D., is Senior Consultant with the National Association for the Education of Young Children (NAEYC) in Washington, DC, and is an Affiliate Faculty Member in Applied Developmental Psychology at George Mason University. She consults with NAEYC, the World Bank, Save the Children, the Families and Work Institute, the National Center for Children in Poverty, and others on early childhood issues. A former preschool and kindergarten teacher and child care director, as NAEYC's Associate Executive Director for Professional Development Marilou helped revise standards for early childhood professional preparation and worked on accreditation and national recognition for 2- and 4-year higher education programs. She has also helped develop position statements on early learning standards, early childhood mathematics, and curriculum/assessment/program evaluation. Before joining NAEYC's staff, she was Professor and Chair of the University of Delaware's Department of Individual and Family Studies. A former editor of *Early Childhood Research Quarterly*, Marilou was also a former Society for Research in Child Development (SRCD) Policy Fellow in the U.S. Department of Education's National Institute on Early Childhood Development and Education. She recently co-chaired SRCD's Committee on Policy and Communications and is a member of numerous national advisory boards in the early childhood field. Her research and publications have emphasized young children's emotional development, parents' and teachers' beliefs and educational practices, issues in linking research with practice, and early childhood teacher preparation.